FRANCESCO CLEMENTE A PRIVATE GEOGRAPHY

MARY BOONE GALLERY
2010

ARTHUR C. DANTO

FRANCESCO CLEMENTE A PRIVATE GEOGRAPHY

CHARTA

CONTENTS

FLIGHTS AND PERCHINGS: FRANCESCO CLEMENTE'S RECENT WORKS ON PAPER: NEW YORK, FRENCH WEST INDIES, BRAZIL AND INDIA

ARTHUR C. DANTO

Earlier this year, the artist Francesco Clemente spent a period of time in L'Orient, a site in the French West Indies, where he painted five luminous and witty watercolor illustrations for a book I would wager that few who see them at Mary Boone's uptown gallery this fall will have read: Attar's *The Conference of the Birds*. Attar was a Sufi poet, and *The Conference of the Birds* is a book of poems originally written in Persian, the subject of which is an allegorical journey made by thirty birds in search of enlightenment, led by a Hoopoe as their guide. (The Hoopoe, *Upupa epops*, is the king of the birds in Aristophanes' comedy *The Birds*, for those that know they have come across Hoopoes somewhere in their education.) The inventive quintet is exemplary of the virtues of watercolor, that neglected medium. In one, the leader has landed on a poised arrow, with the insouciance of a street pigeon. The fluid background has the color of urine and overall look of one of Andy Warhol's oxidation paintings. In a companion piece, the enlightenment-seekers are perched in the nested locks of a beautiful youth with opulent lips, sleeping or slain it is difficult to say, since his eyes are closed. I cannot do justice to the other three, though I will mention a plumed serpent slithering past a clock set at five minutes to six. Such clocks did not exist in Attar's time, so the picture tells us something it could not have told Attar's first readers, the question being what?

*

In 2006, 2007 and 2008, Clemente spent an extended period in Rio de Janeiro and in Bahia, executing a series of richly shaded studies of rituals performed and ritual objects used by "Actors of the Terreiro"—officials in what has evolved out of the Candomblé religion, carried to Brazil by African slaves in the 16th century, and since then mixed with the arts of native Brazilian witch doctors and medicine men and women, themselves inflected by Christian iconography. The result is a highly syncretic orthodoxy, whose practice was banned until 1970 and has since then flourished. Its ceremonies are conducted in Yoruban. The typical Candomblé deities are Brazilian-African-Christian hybrids, for whom the labor of devotion is a fairly full-time occupation, in terms of cuisine, laundered garments and rites. Candomblé is very much a lived religion, as the nightly drumming in Bahia attests, but for the most part it is open to tourists, making it a significant part of Brazil's economy.

The drawings are not easily interpreted. Some seem to show straightforward domestic duties, like sewing buttons in a painting that has the look of Léger, or washing a white garment by hand. There is a ritual object similar to a fetish one has seen in anthropological collections, in which nail upon nail is driven into a block of wood, which evokes voodoo associations. In other cases there appear to be martyrdoms, in which deities, wearing cardinal hats, are gods that help with certain diseases like smallpox, or leprosy overseen by Saint Lazarus. The saints are surrounded by offerings, much as one would see in the Church of Vierzehnheiligen, as messages of gratitude or hope. There are chains, ropes and candles as symbols of suffering that have found their way into worship since the Council of Trent and the Counter-Reformation, instruments of torment, but also objects of beautification and glorification. Sacrifice is a major transaction, since the gods swap favors for treats, even, or especially, in Candomblé.

*

In 2008, Clemente undertook a major endeavor, portraying eight of what I have called the Super Sopranos, in that season singing in the Metropolitan Opera. None of these portraits is in the show at Boone, since they were painted on canvas and have a beautful book of their own, but the following year he portrayed himself three times in the form of collaged maps from various regions at various periods, which suggests a certain migratory character that certainly belongs to this artist's mode of being. "When we take a general view of the wonderful stream of our consciousness, what strikes us first is this different pace of its parts. Like a bird's life, it seems to be made of an alternation of flights and perchings," wrote William James in a famous passage in his pioneering work *Principles of Psychology* from 1890. It is as though Clemente realized that he had been in flight since he first left Italy, at the age of 21, when he took flight from the Italian art world in a passage to India, anticipating the epic journey he was to portray on Orient Point years later. The maps were perchings, landing fields, collaged as if he were made of charts as his essence. I don't see Afghanistan. Though he trekked his way there with his mentor, Alighiero e Boetti, but perhaps that remarkable artist belongs in Torino. Sicily overlaps Central Park, separated by the East River from the Golfo di Napoli, whose place names I can identify: Torre Annunciata, Vico Equense, Sorrento and of course the Isle of Capri—all great perching places. I was struck by the artist's knowledge that today Columbia University occupies what had once been the Bloomingdale Insane Asylum, and that the River Ganges with its *ghats* figure in two of the maps. But after all, the anticipation of death is one good reason for checking things out in Bahia and Rio, or wherever the drums beat and the fragrant scent of grilled meats curls its way upward where the gods perch, hungering for something solid.

*

The concluding suite of paintings was in fact the first one made, a delicious sequence of the 21 forms of love—not the 21 acts or positions of love, which of course belongs to the Kama Sutra. Clemente showed me these four-by-six-inch drawings between the pages of a bound book, as if a special deck of cards for playing twenty-one. Twenty-one is a notable number, the age at which one attains maturity and casts one's first ballot. It is a kind of numerological number. What gives twenty-one its distinctiveness among numbers is the kind of question one imagines Indian mathematicians would have given thought to. One always thinks of Ramanujan's response to G.H. Hardy's claim that 1729—the number of the taxi he took to visit the genius—is a dull number. No, Hardy, he replied, it is indeed a very interesting number, mathematically, being the smallest number representable in two different ways as a sum of two cubes. Paradoxically, I know of nothing that mathematically interesting about the number 21. Yet 21 seems associated with the problems of love, perhaps because 1 + 1 gives birth to 1. If there were something that interesting in 21 and love, though, the Indians would have taught it to us. So I'll suppose that Clemente perched in India for three weeks—21 days—and put his days to good use by dedicating them to love.

The work was done in Varanasi, to use the name now given to Benares, whose map turns up twice in Clemente's self-portraits, showing the *ghats* used in funerary ceremonies. I imagine him doing one of these love images each day. The suite begins with Krishna's head being held against the right breast of what I would surmise is a *gopi*—one of the cow-herding women he frolicked with. Krishna's body is nowhere to be seen. Lovers exchange gifts, accept flowers from one another, eye a clock impatiently while holding hands, and lie next to one another when passion is spent, or sit alone by the window, gazing at the moonlight on the Ganges. As near as one can make out, the love is between male and female, with the surprising appearance of the female in contemporary western clothing—an orange top over a short yellow skirt, drawn as Art Deco figures. One can use the suite as a flip book to keep track of the changes. There is a wonderful image of a couple under an umbrella, marching past a pair of overlapping hearts, deep in conversational animation. It's not the kind of image anyone associated with Benares. Clemente's well-known irony finds an ideal outlet in drawing the faces—and bodies!—of love in a city devoted to leaving one body for another that one's karma has preshaped.

*

The show ends with everything fitted together as jigsaw pieces in a frame. It looks like the concluding scene of *The Conference of the Birds*, floating on the surface of a river and looking at a rainbow. The rainbow arches over a floating female goddess with long tresses interweaving between the arcs. There is a couple stretched out, body to body, in the upper left piece, sharing their space with a bird. The upper right jigsaw piece shows an eye, and shows what the eye sees without giving us a hint of what it is. Between the legs of the goddess, a couple kisses in the dark. There is a chained couple beneath the goddess's arms. They are chained to opposing walls. Our friend, the yellow snake—now featherless—coils in the lower right corner. It is some kind of cosmology showing the deity as part of the world, a Sufi belief. Human beings are enclosed in darkness but waiting for liberation. It is an extremely ambitious piece of work, 77 by 98 inches, and finished this year. I have not yet done it justice. But a few words from Wikipedia about the epic journey of thirty birds may help us in situating love's place in the geography of enlightenment: The birds must cross seven valleys in order to find the *Simorgh*: *Talab* (Yearning), *Eshq* (Love), *Marifat* (Gnosis), *Istighnah* (Detachment), *Tawheed* (Unity of God), *Hayrat* (Bewilderment) and, finally, *Fuqur* and *Fana* (Selflessness and Oblivion in God). These represent the stations that a Sufi or any individual must pass through to realize the true nature of God. I leave it to the reader to explain why the artist would be certain to make a U-turn back to New York once he attains the station of Love, presumably having no interest in pressing on to Detachment, let alone Bewilderment.

RIO DE JANEIRO / BAHIA • 2006 2007 2008

ACTORS OF THE TERREIRO

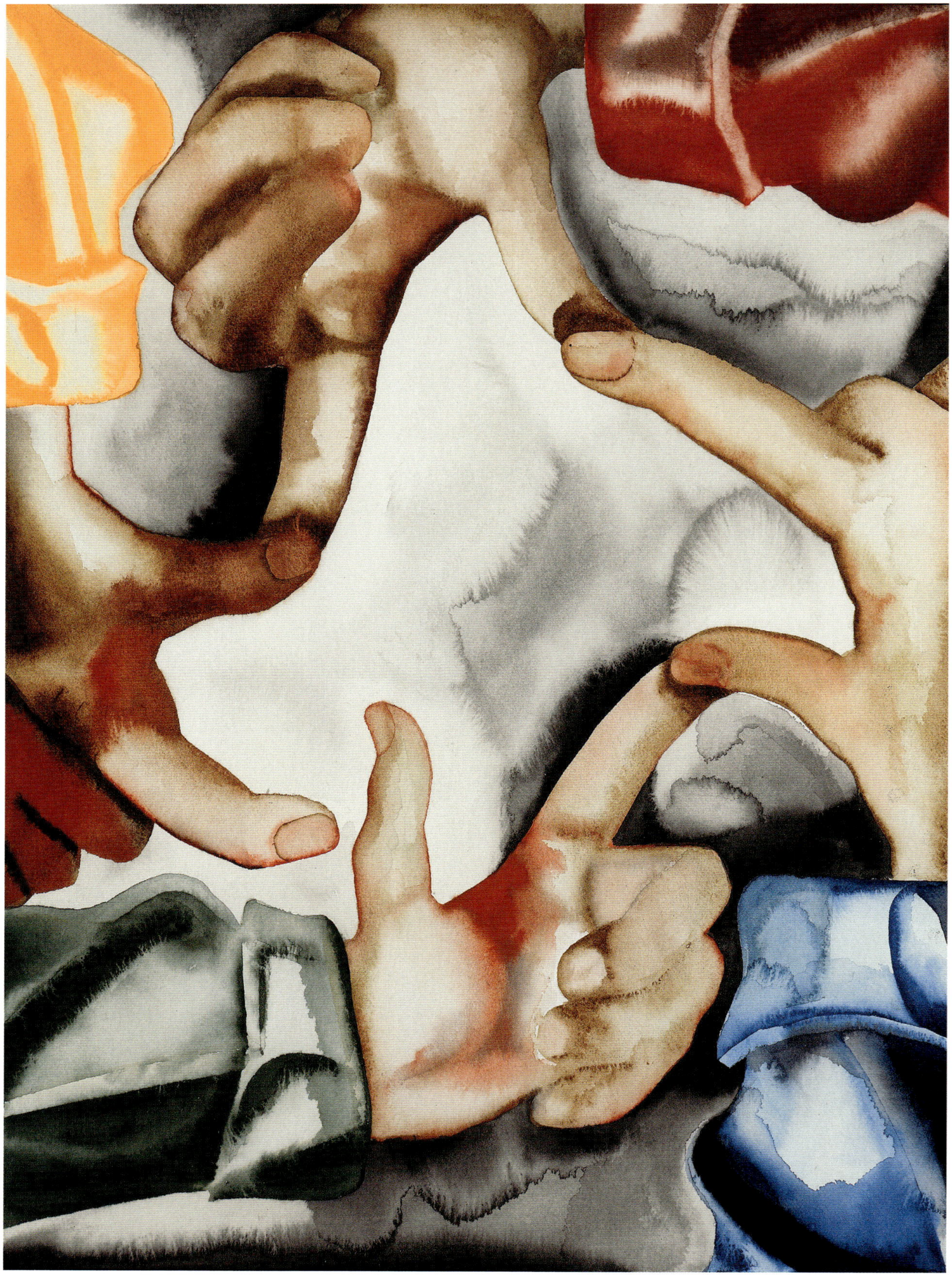

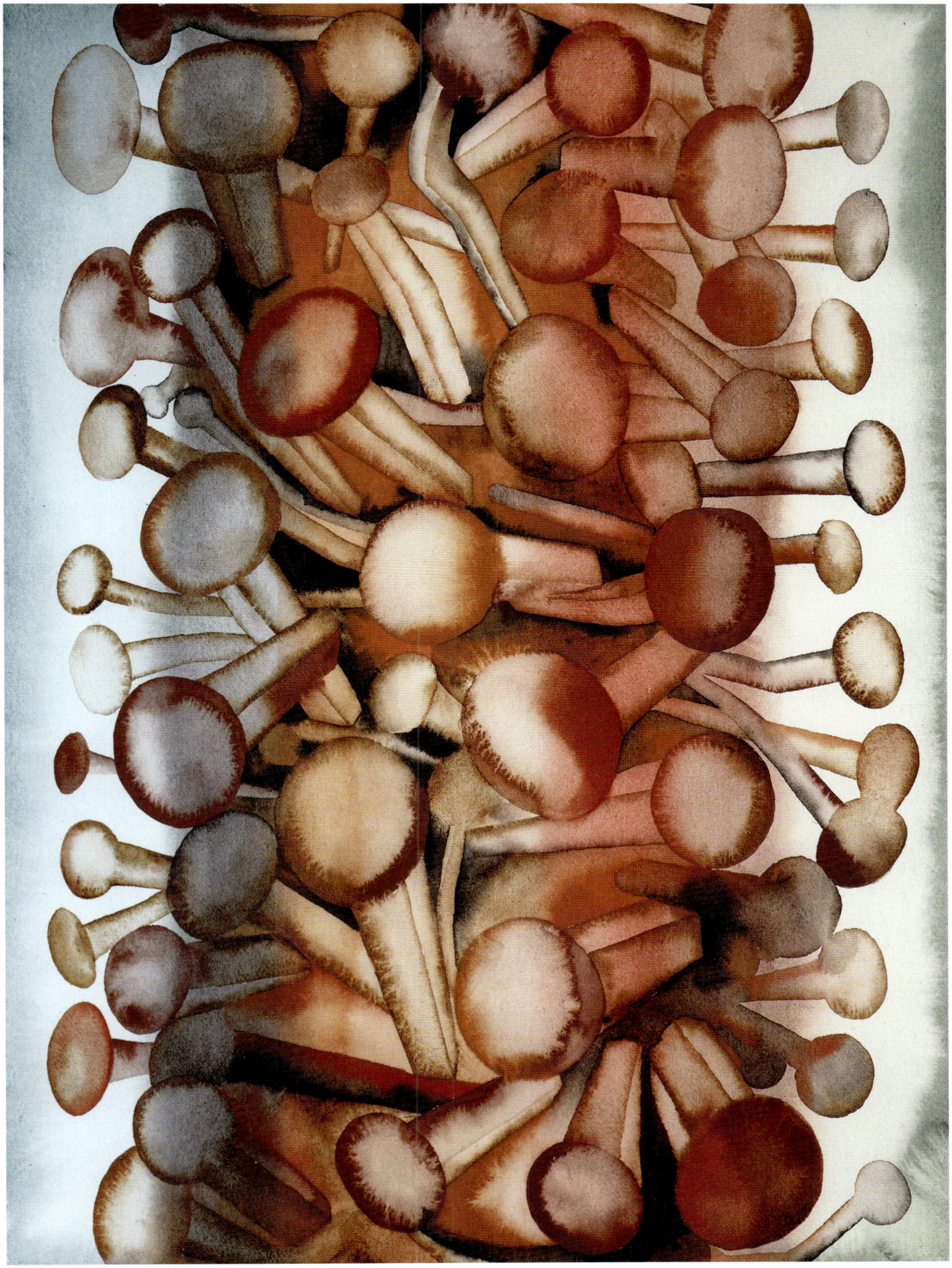

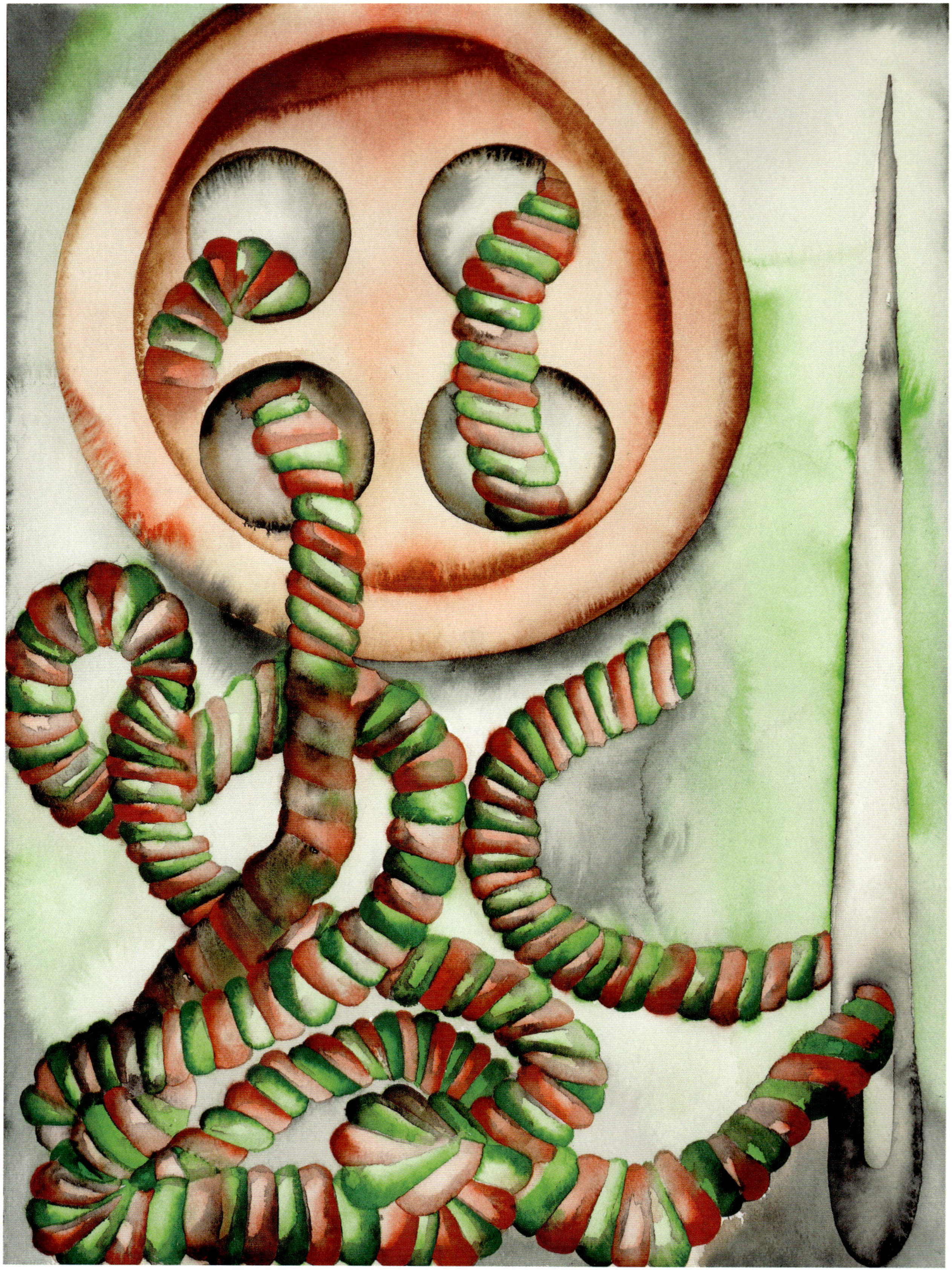

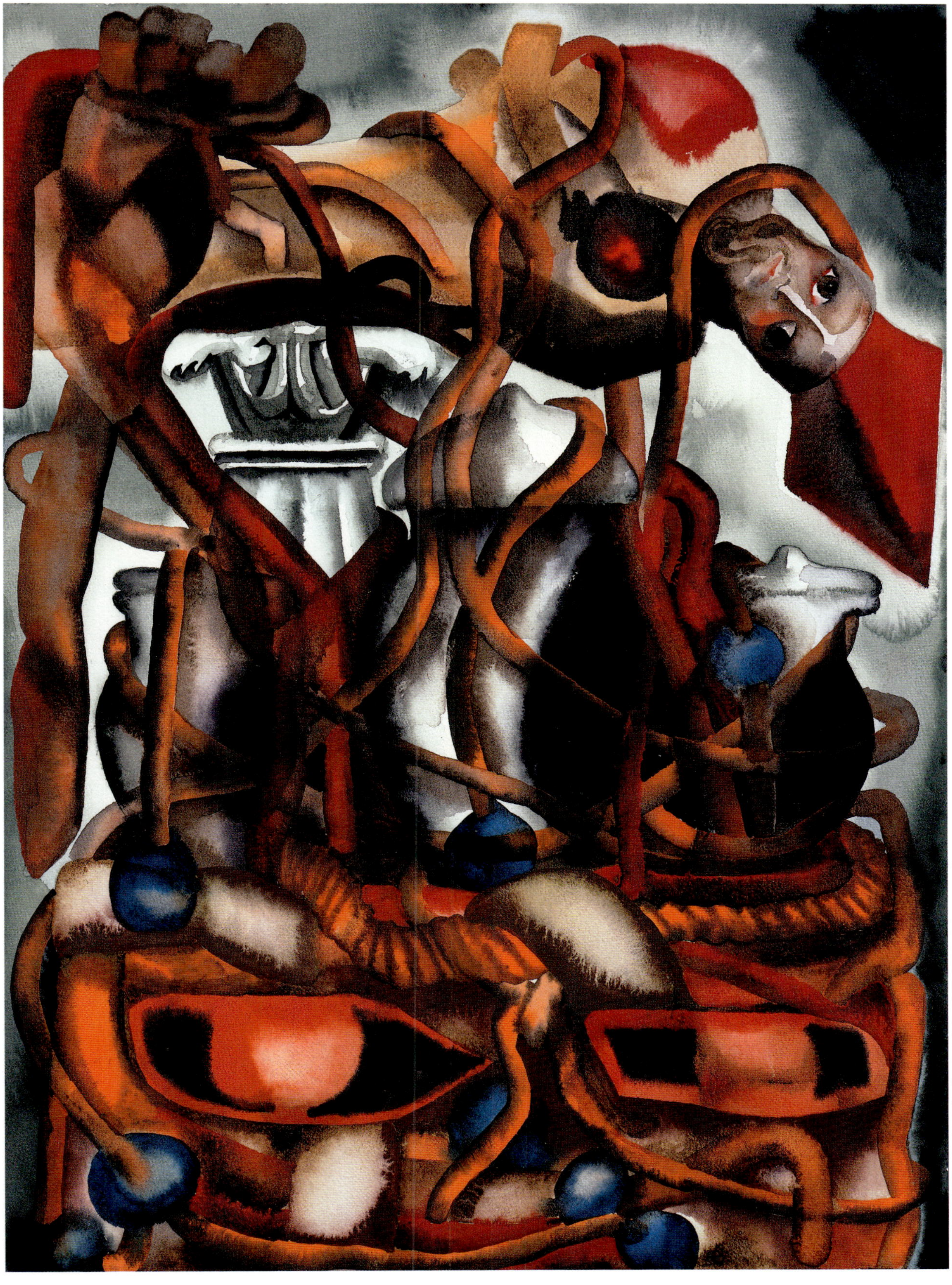

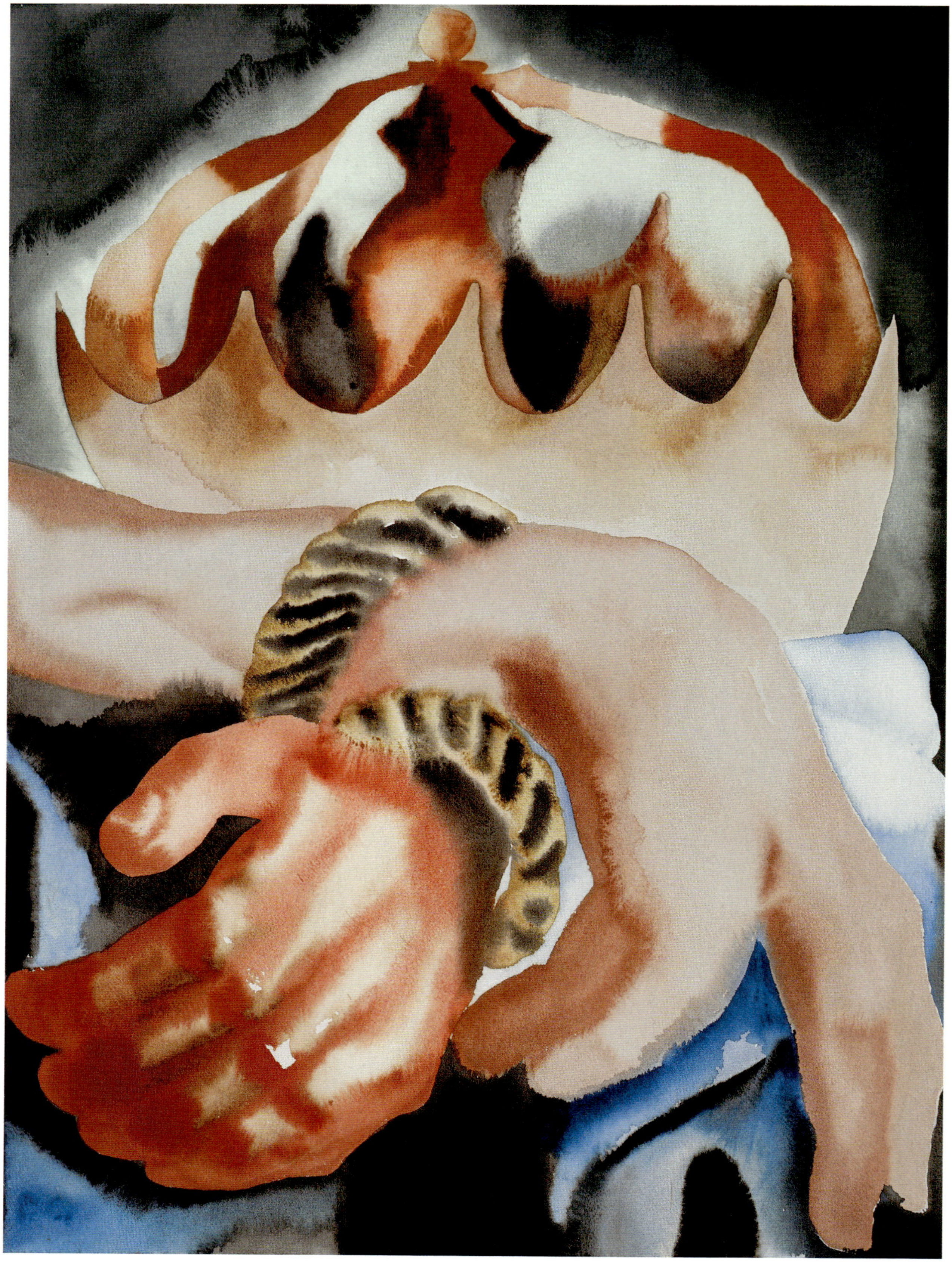

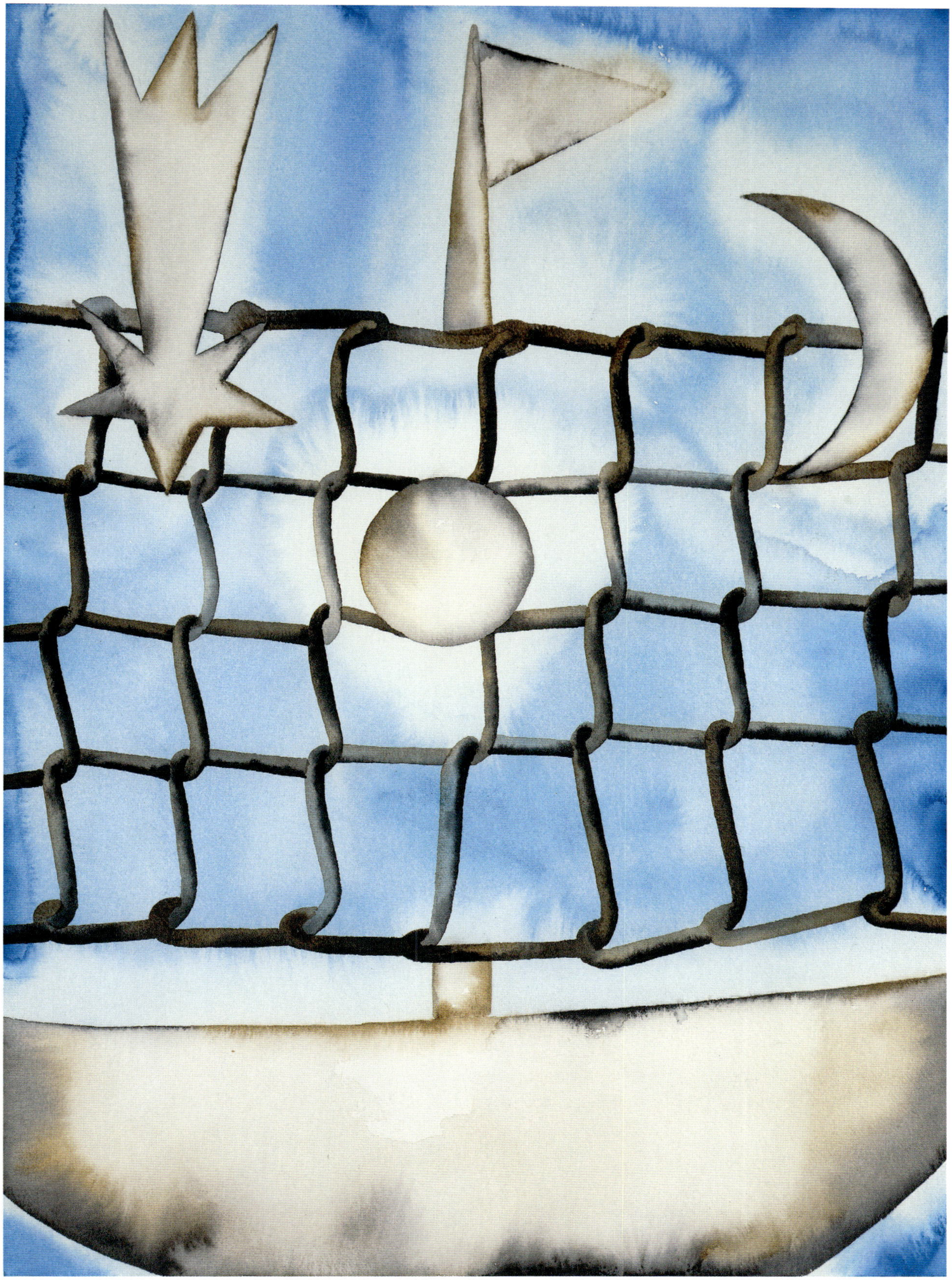

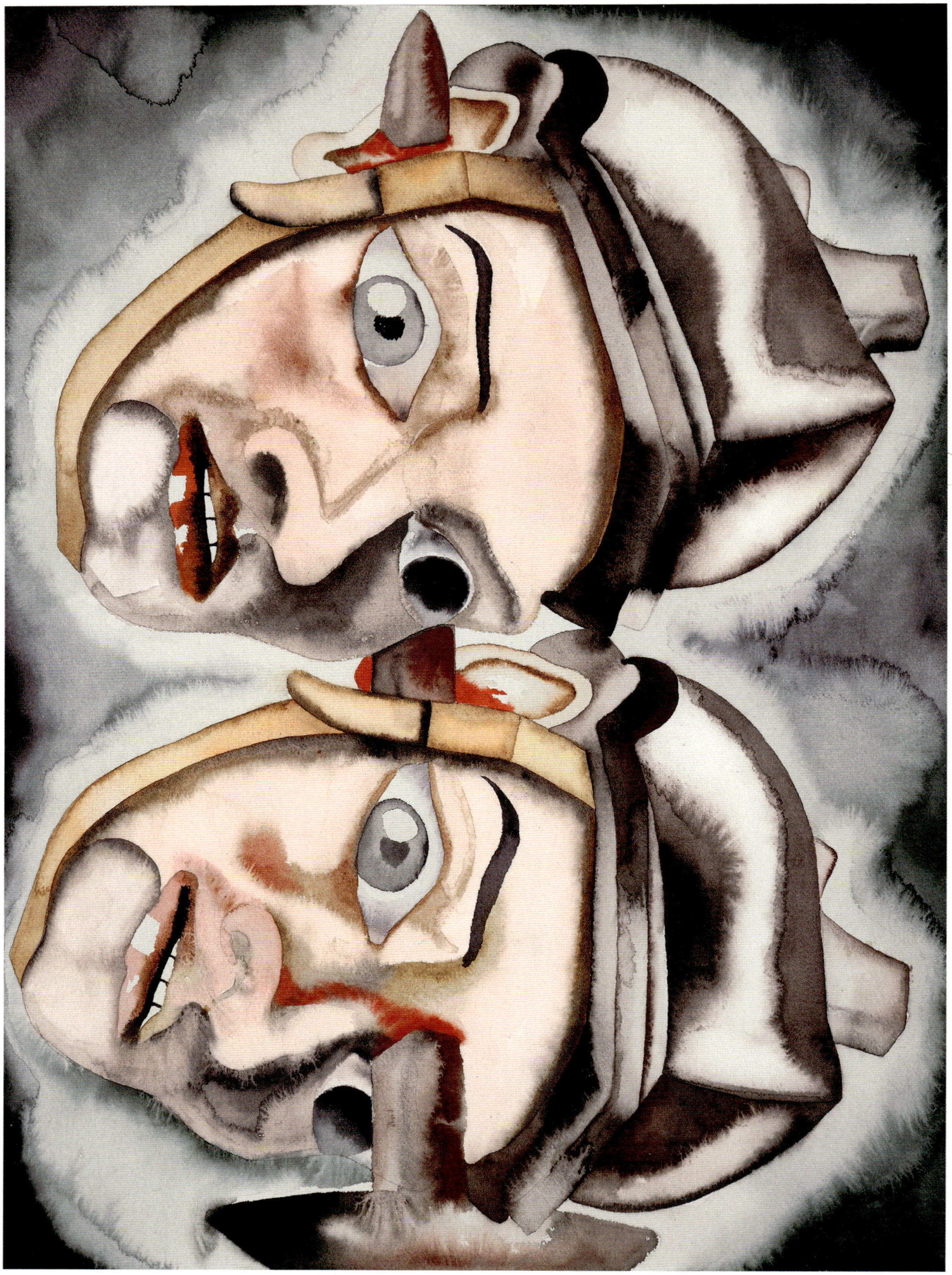

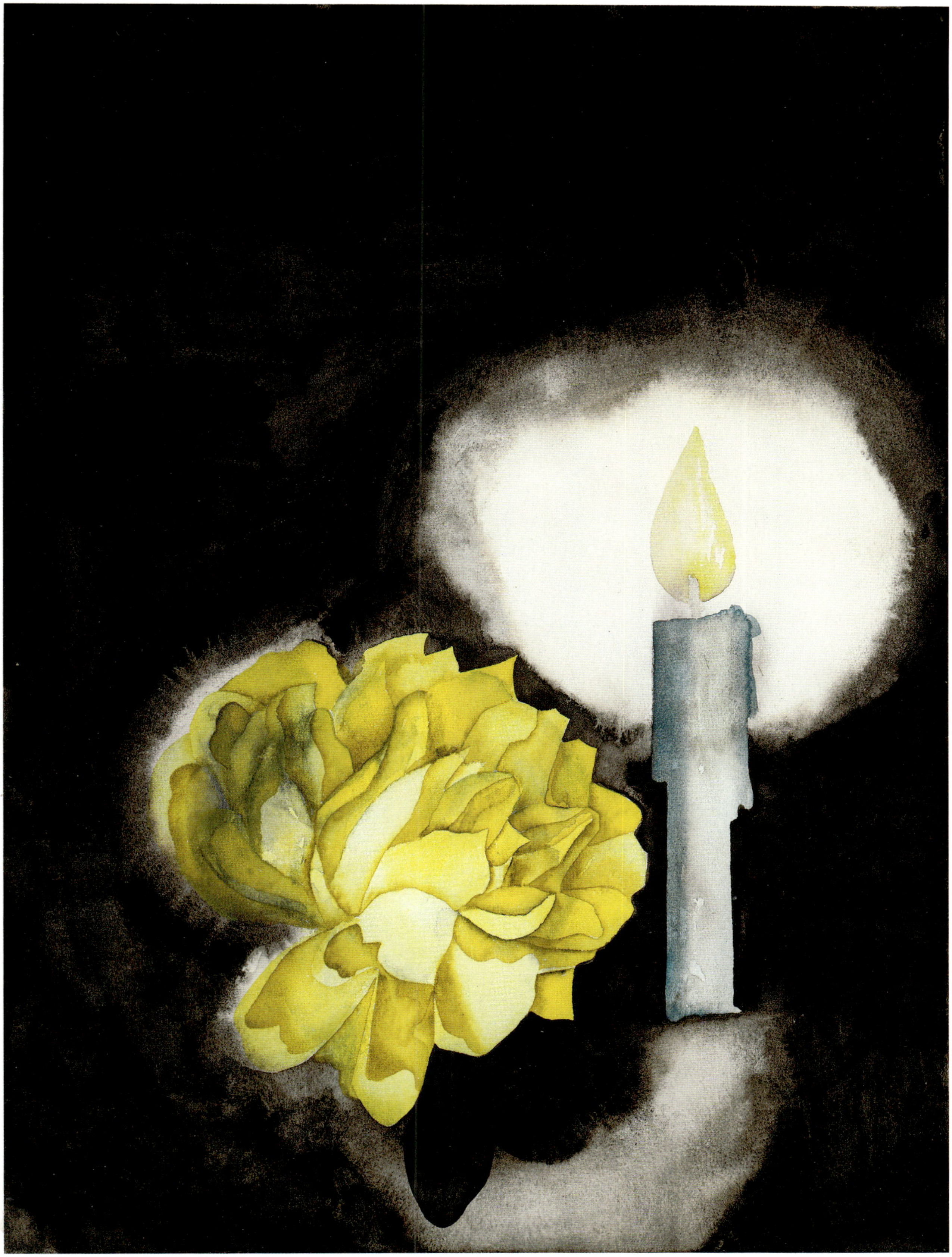

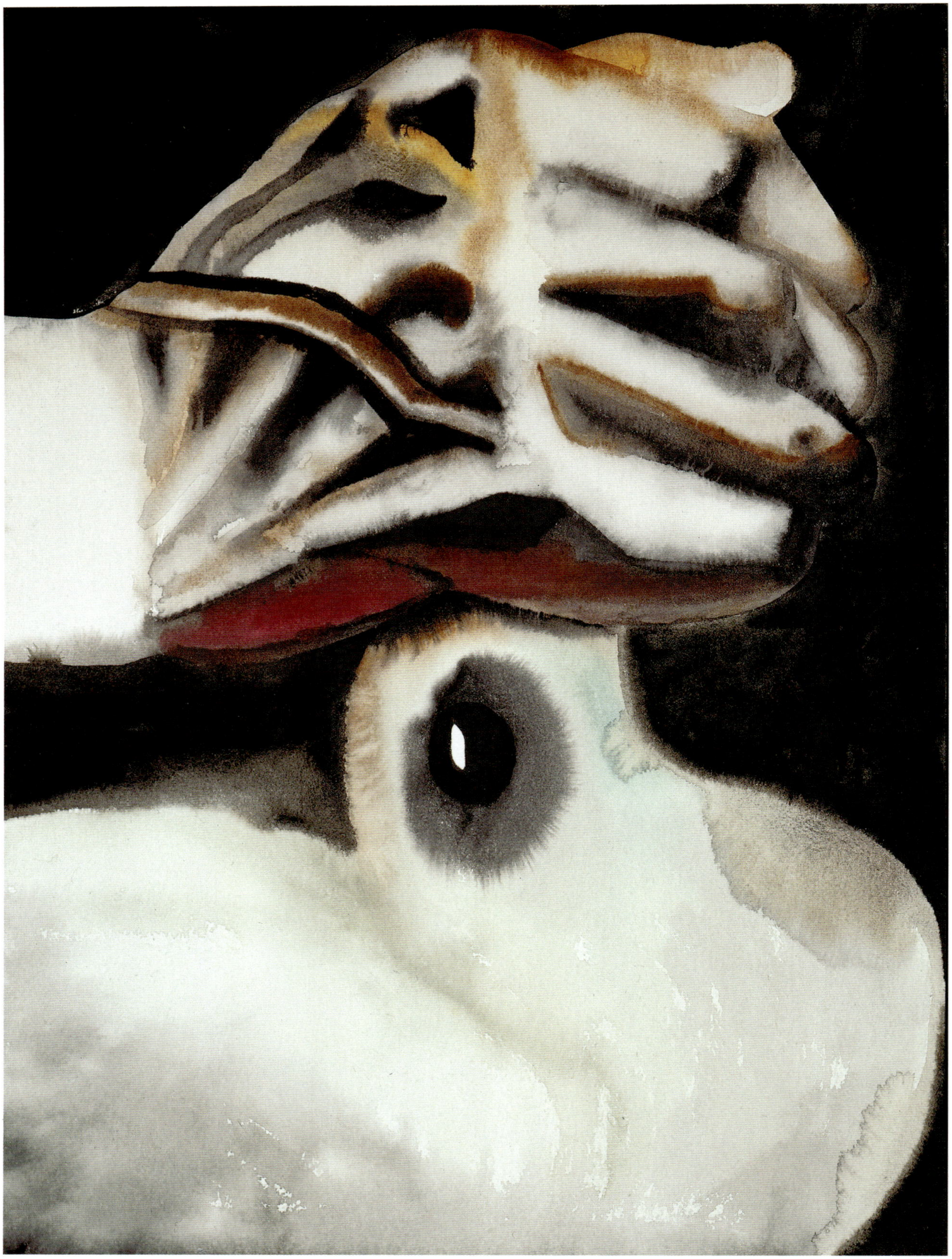

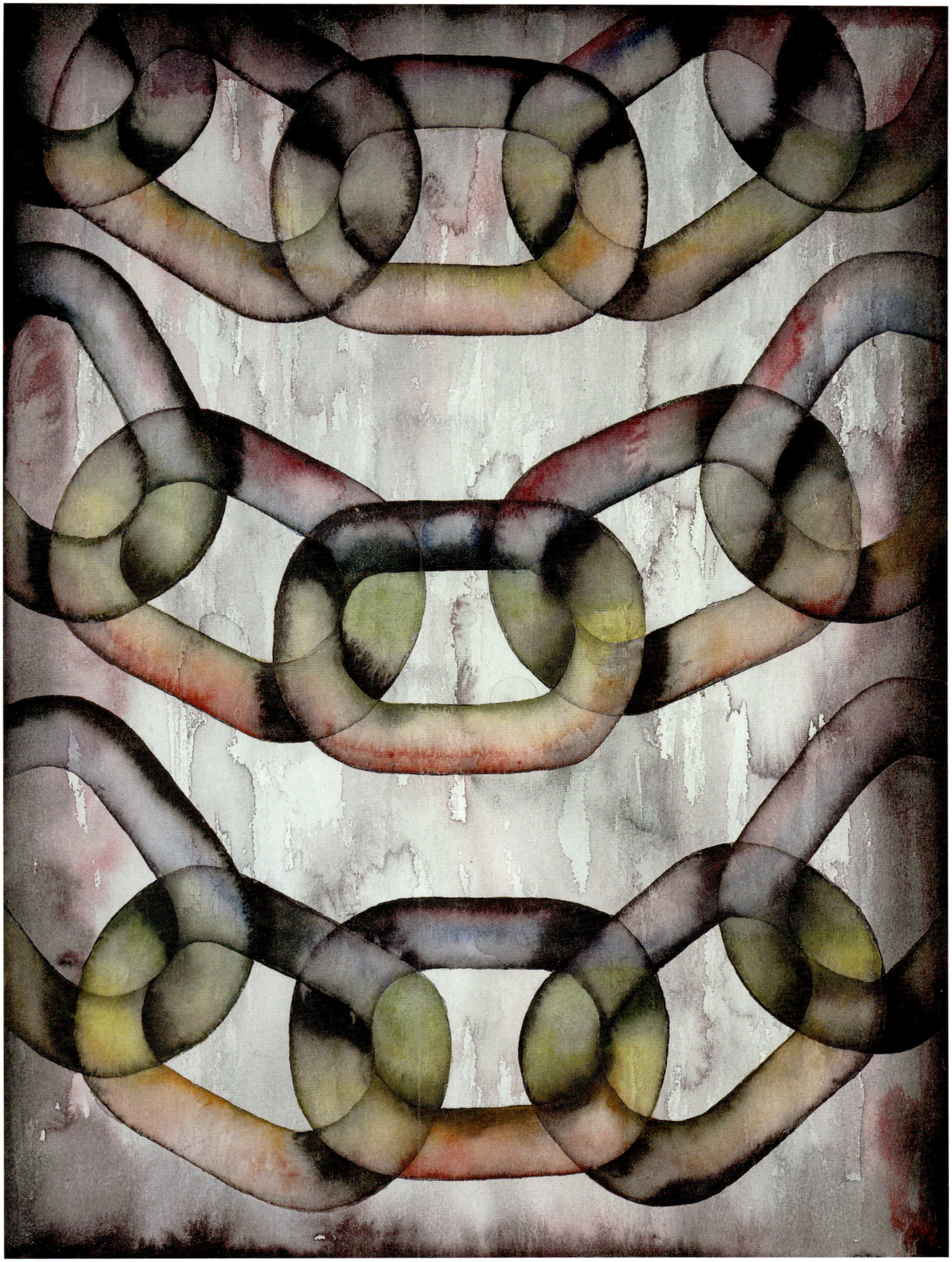

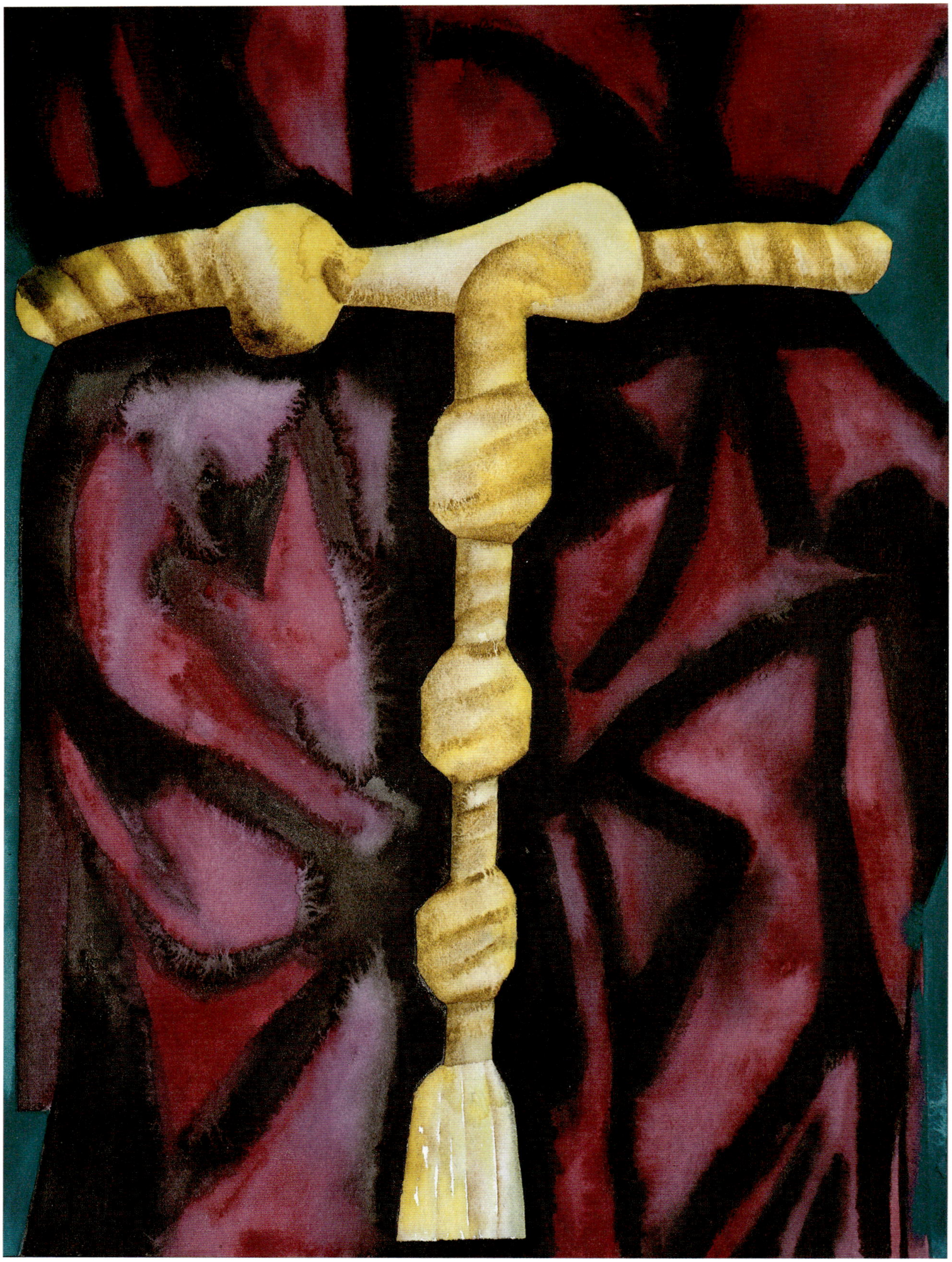

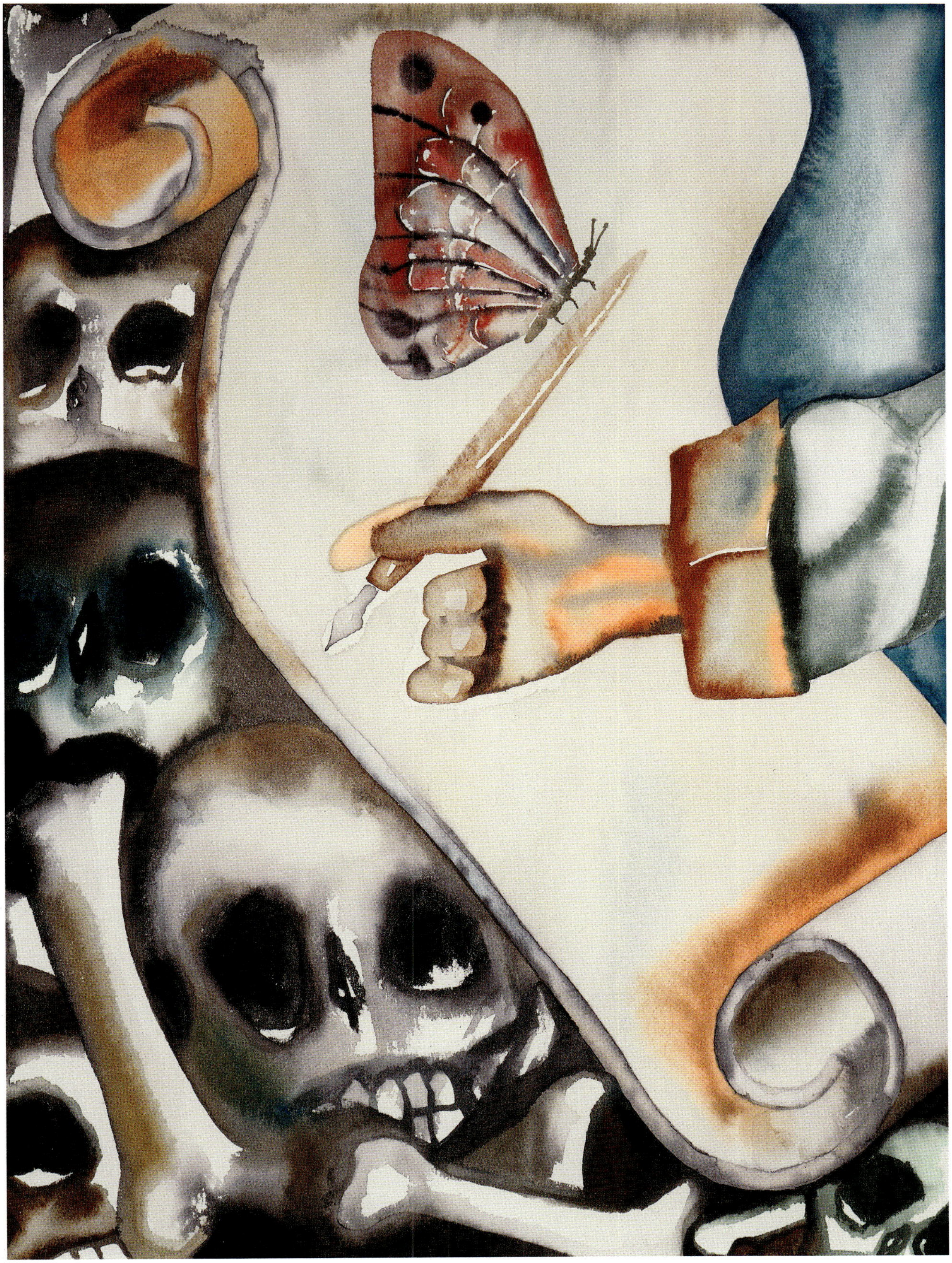

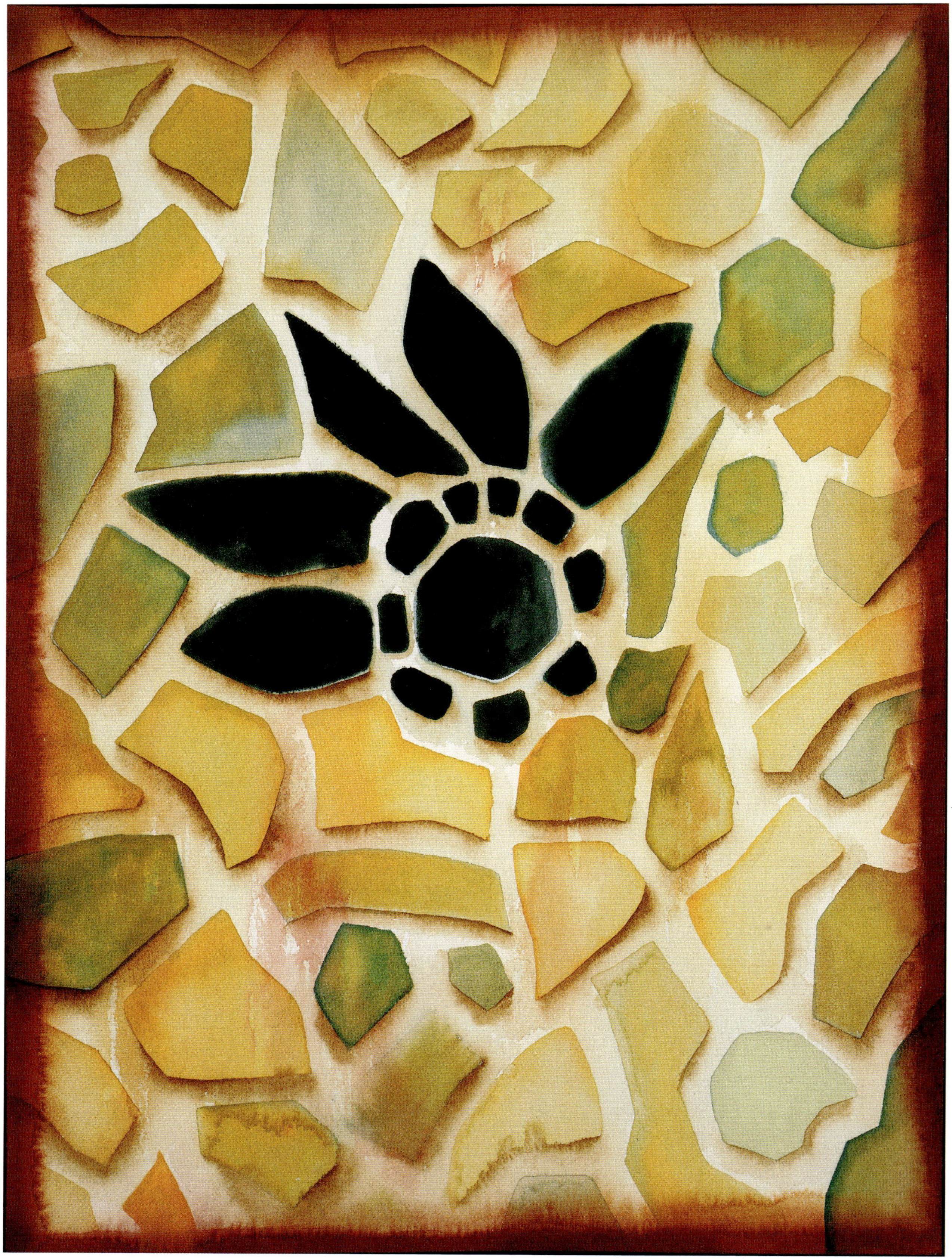

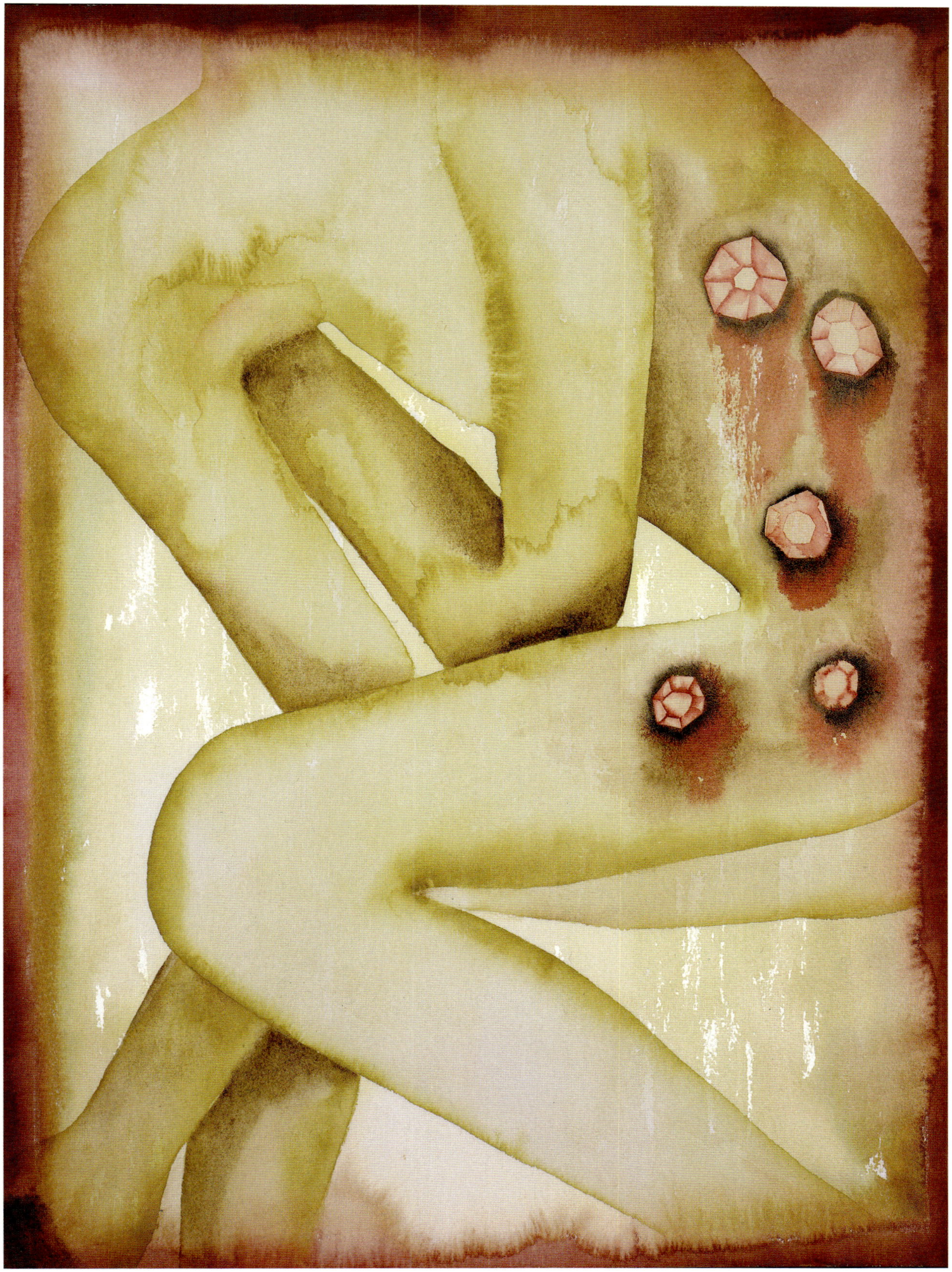

VARANASI • 2008

TWENTY-ONE KINDS OF LOVE

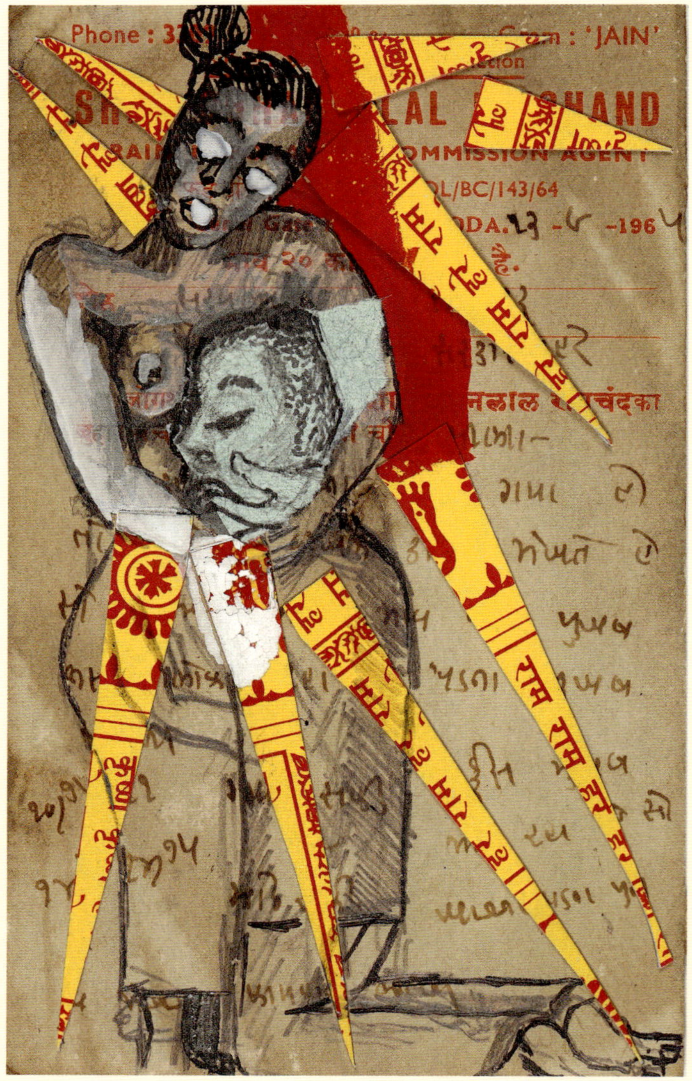
'JAIN'
COMMISSION AGENT

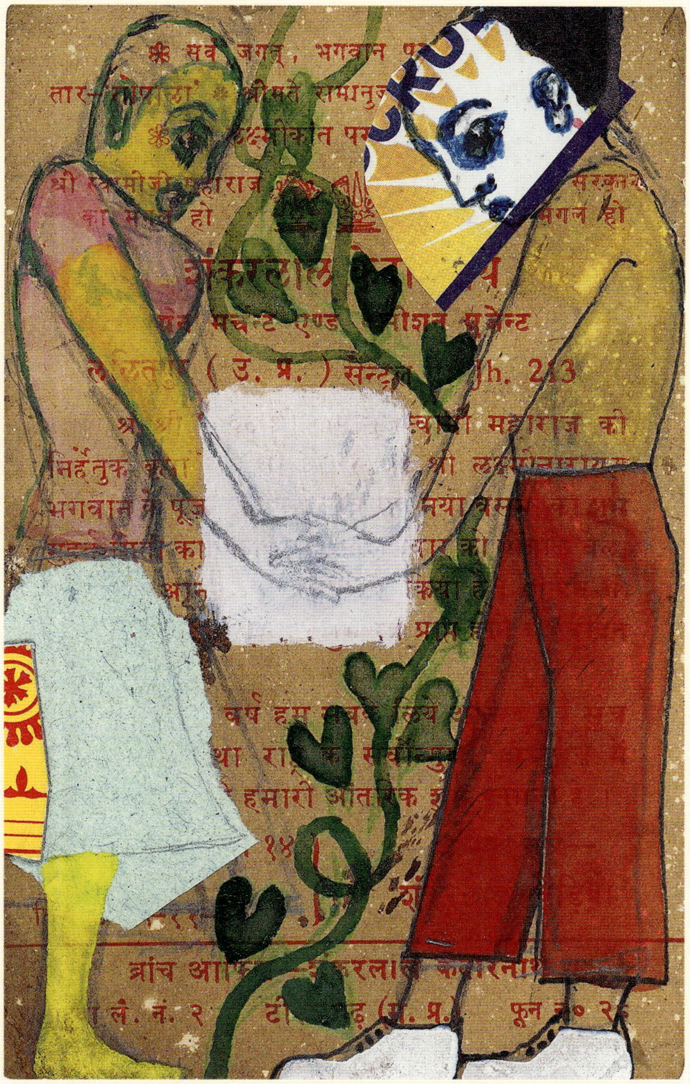

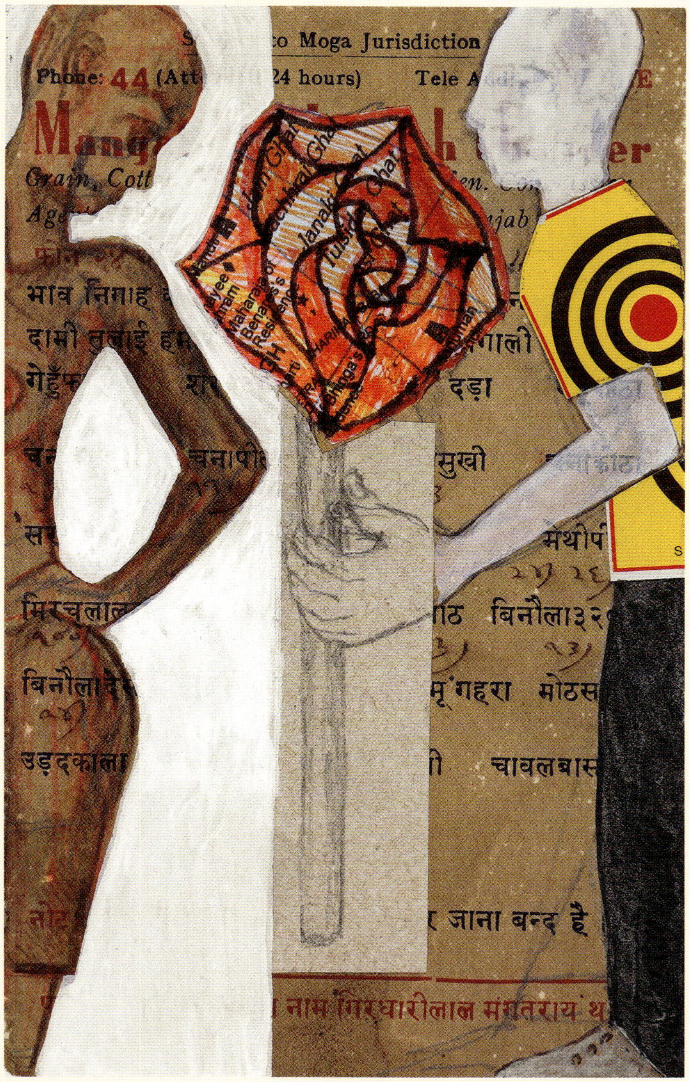
co Moga Jurisdiction
Phone: 44
24 hours)
Grain, Cott
जाना बन्द है
चावलबास

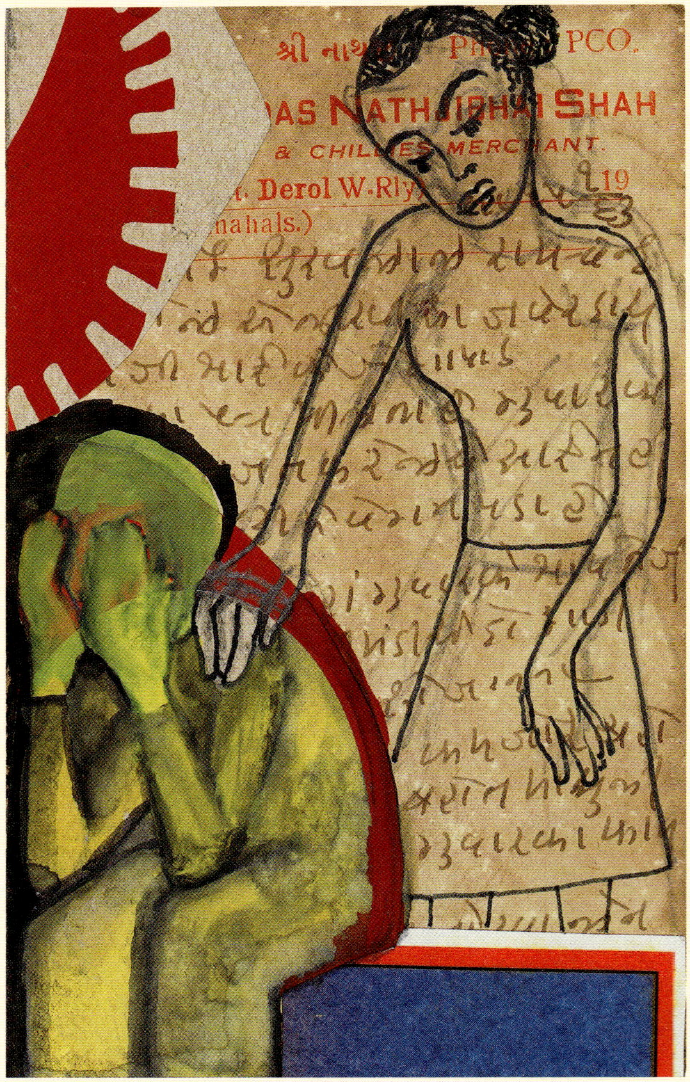
PCO.
SHAH
Derol W.Rly.

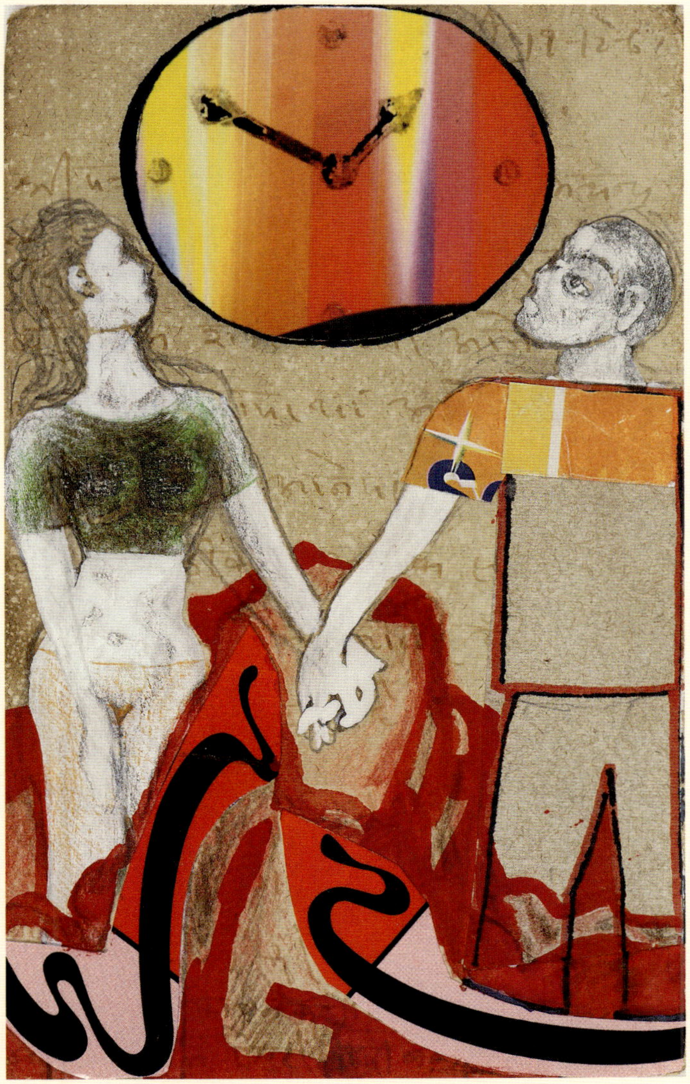

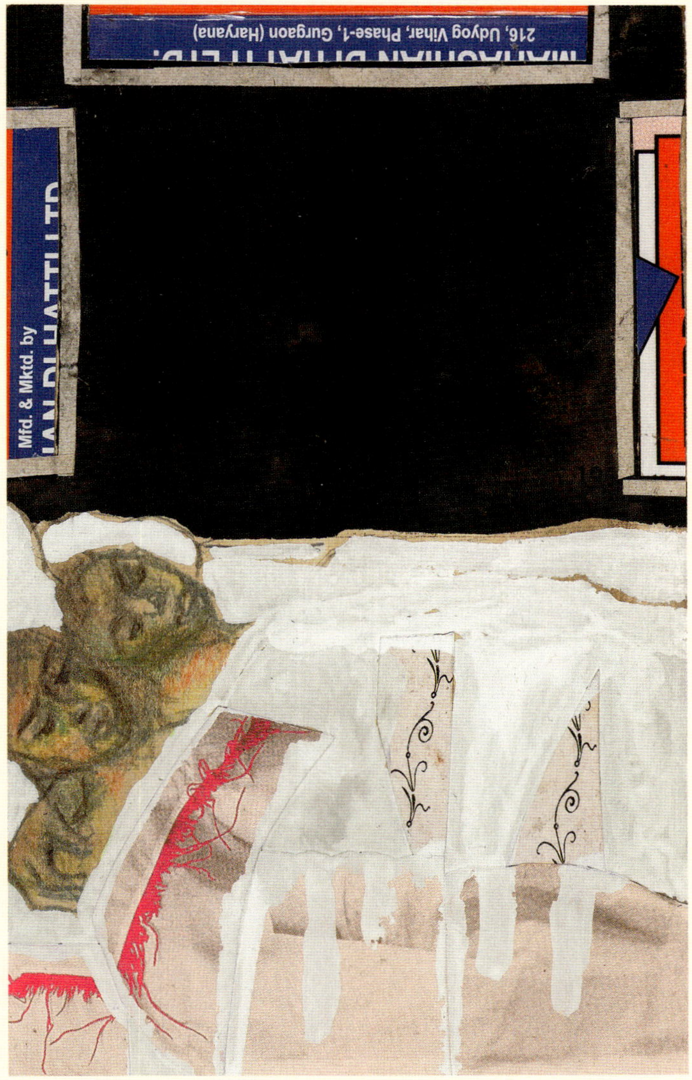
216, Udyog Vihar, Phase-1, Gurgaon (Haryana)
Mfd. & Mktd. by

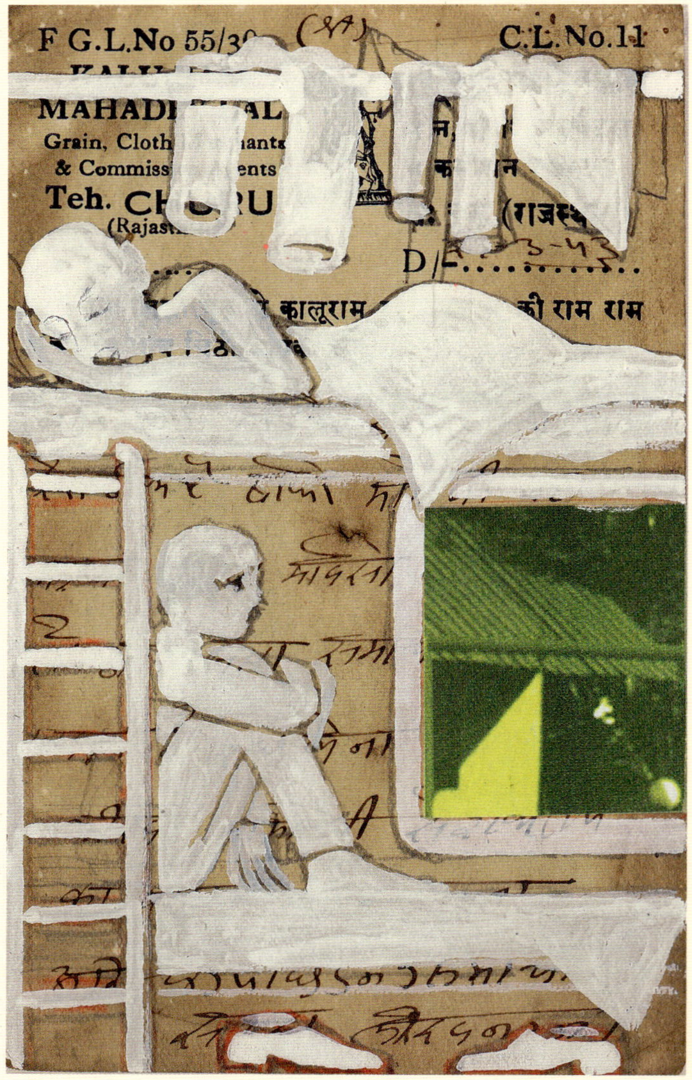
F G.L.No 55/3
C.L.No.11
कालूराम
की राम राम

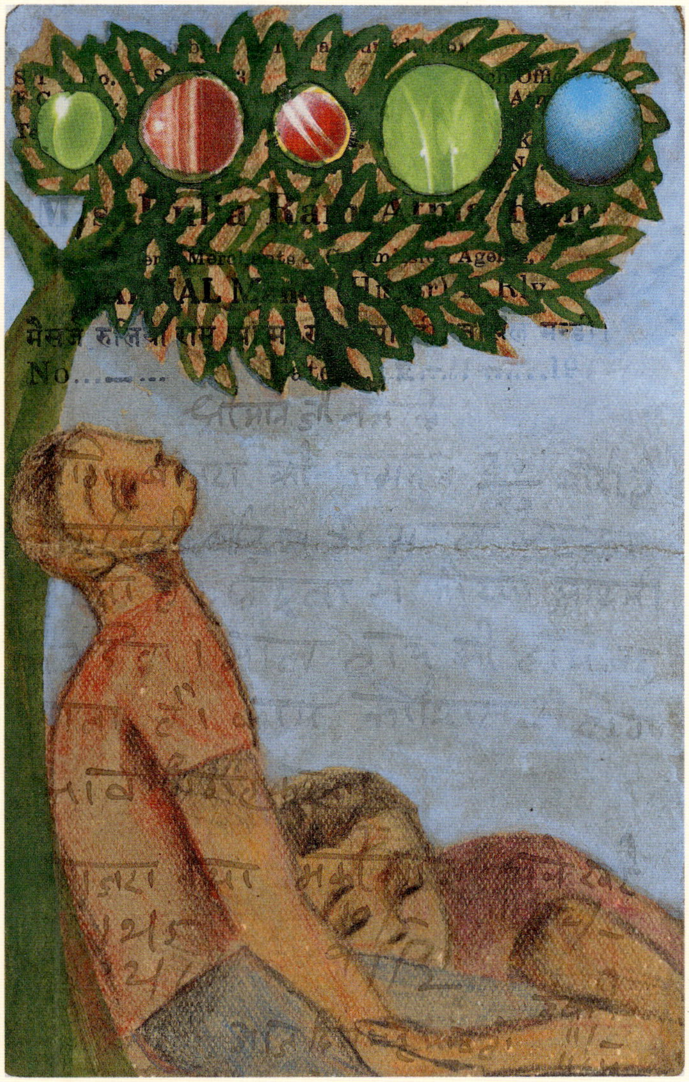

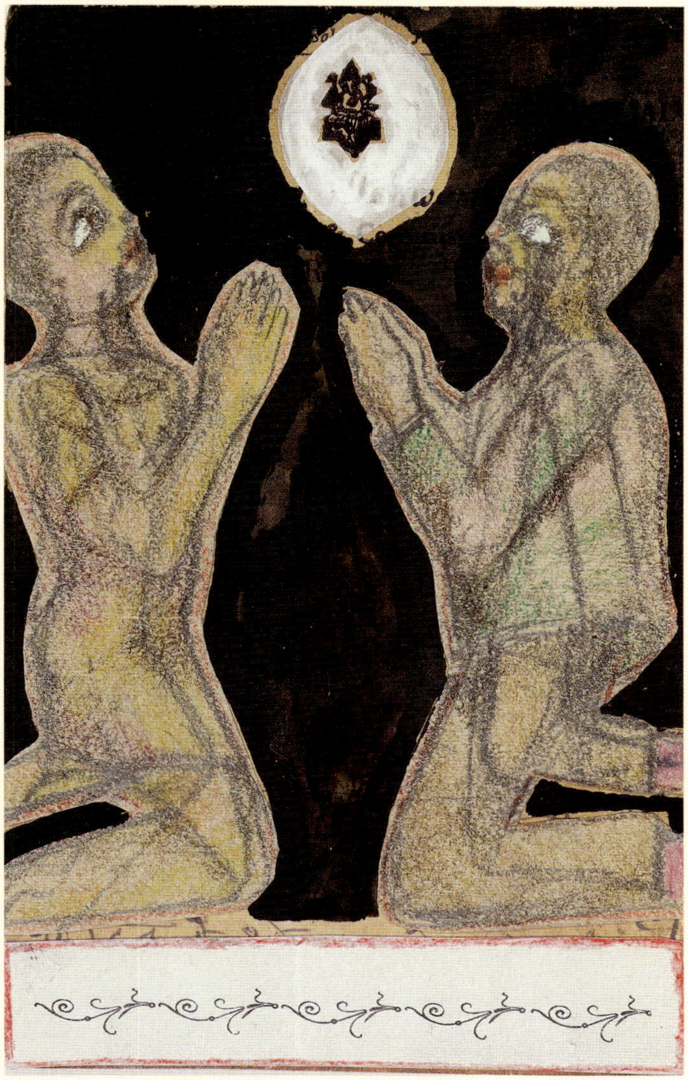

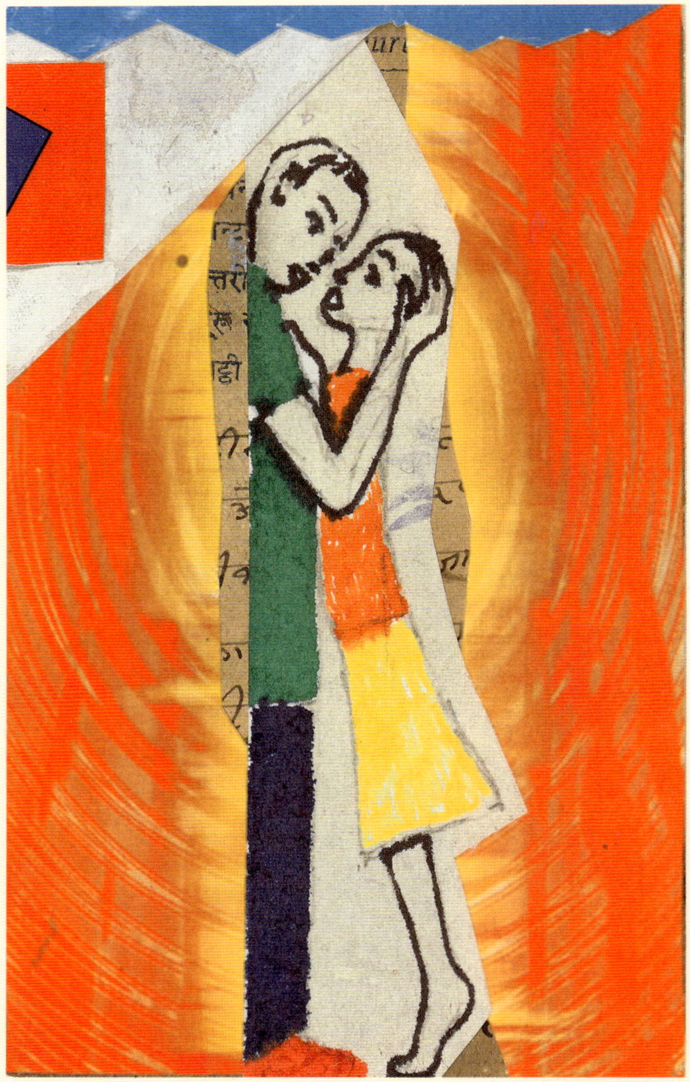

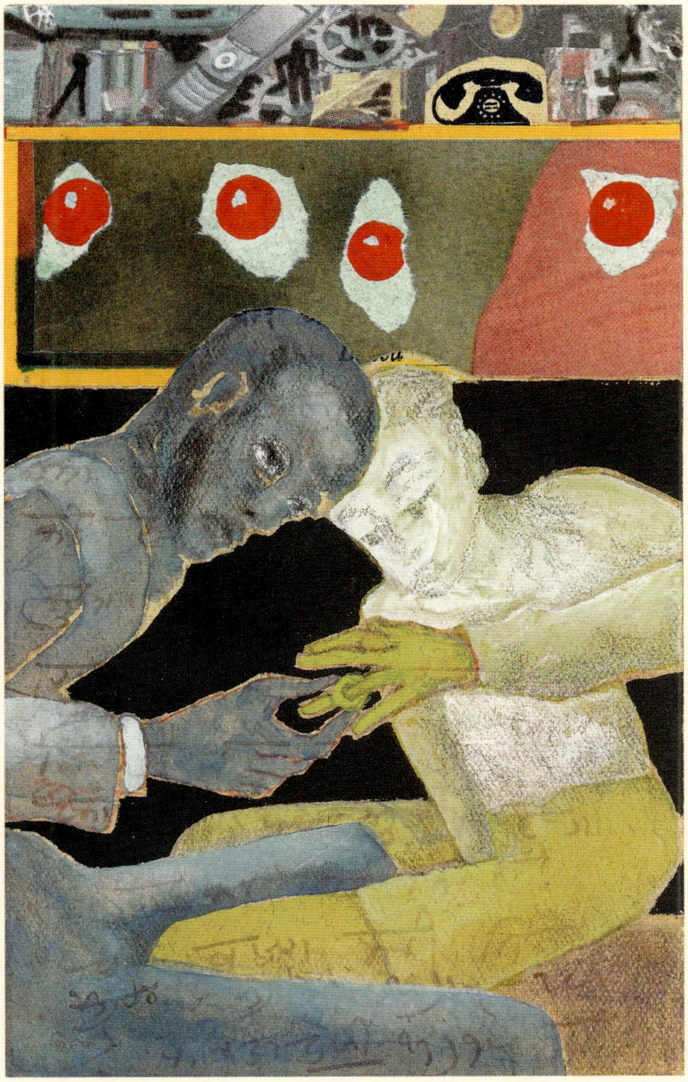

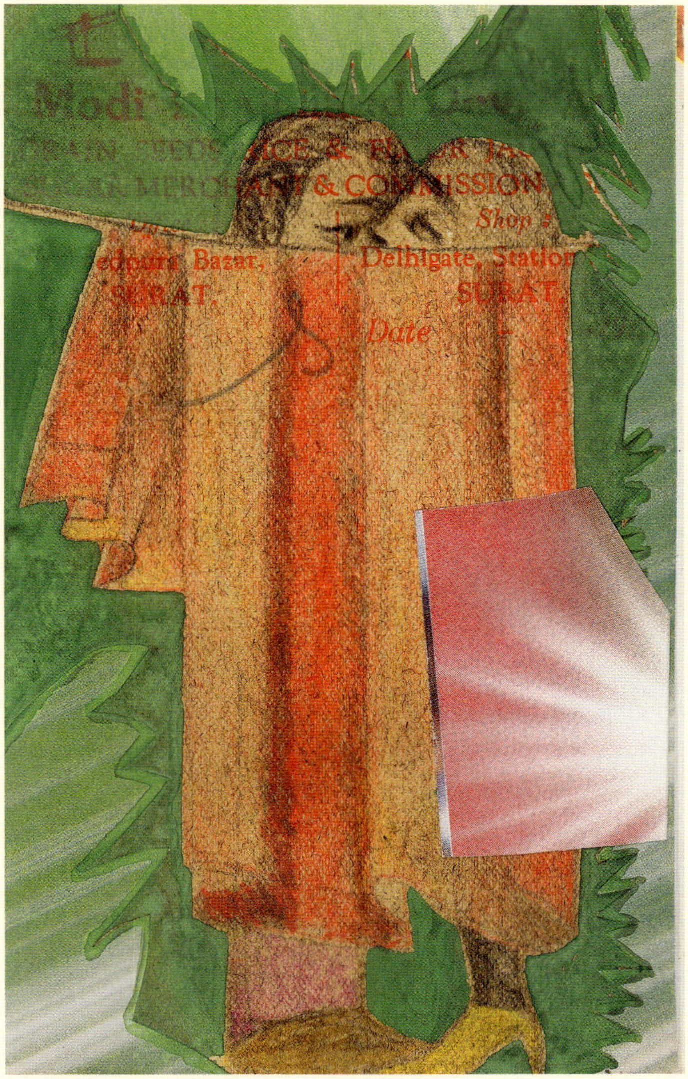
Modi
& COMMISSION
Shop
Bazar,
SURAT.
SURAT.
Date

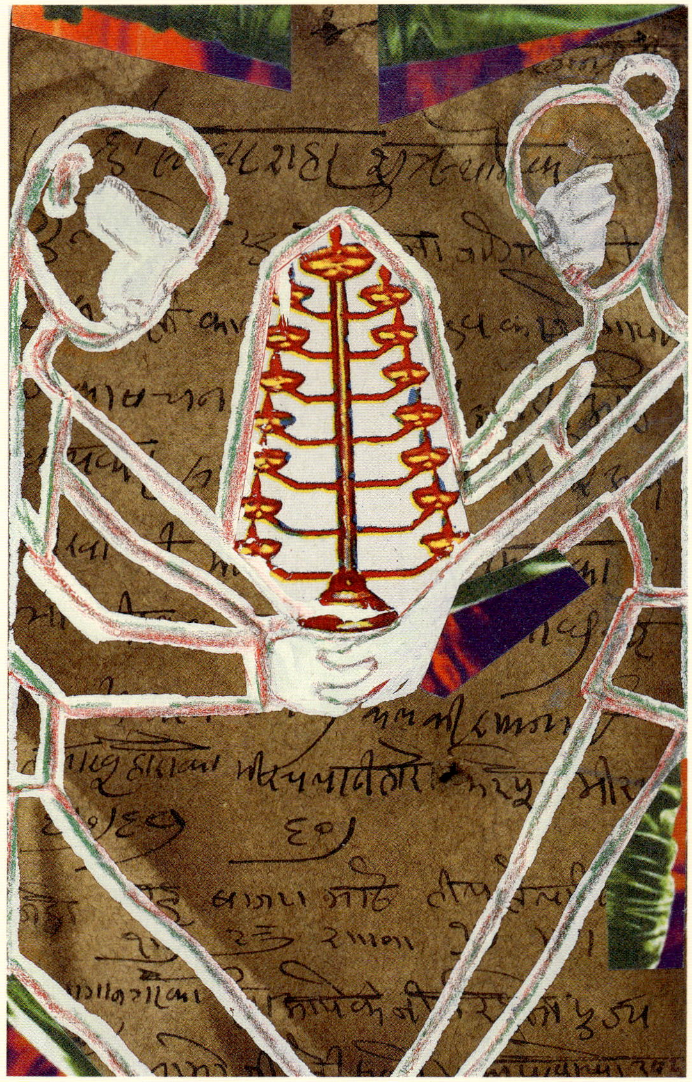

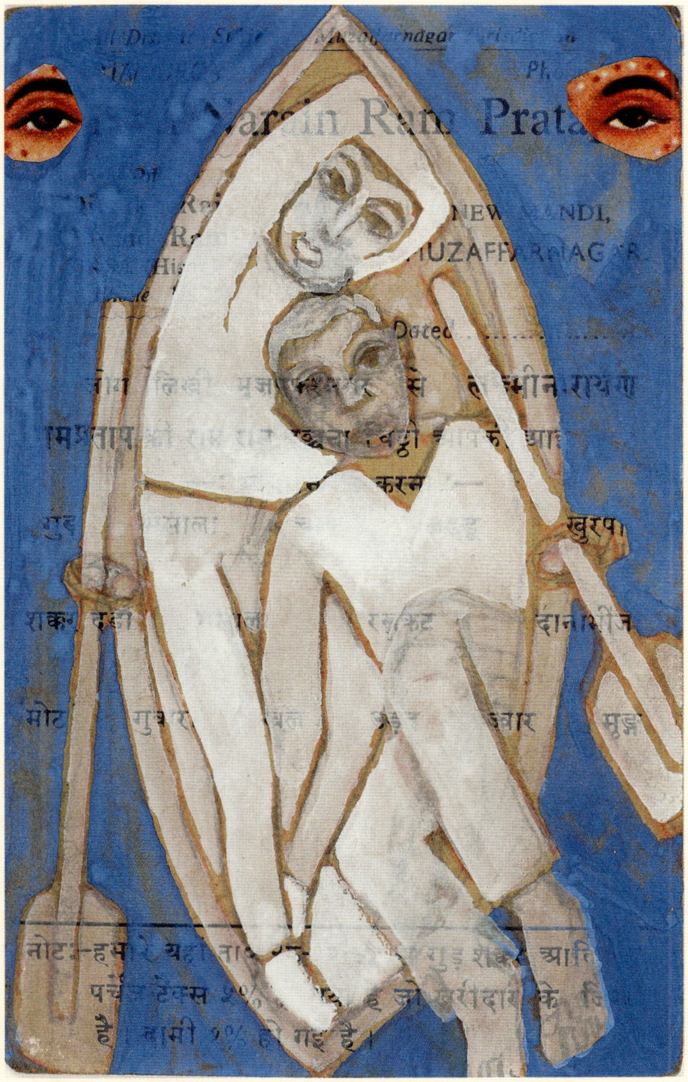
NEW MANDI,
Dated

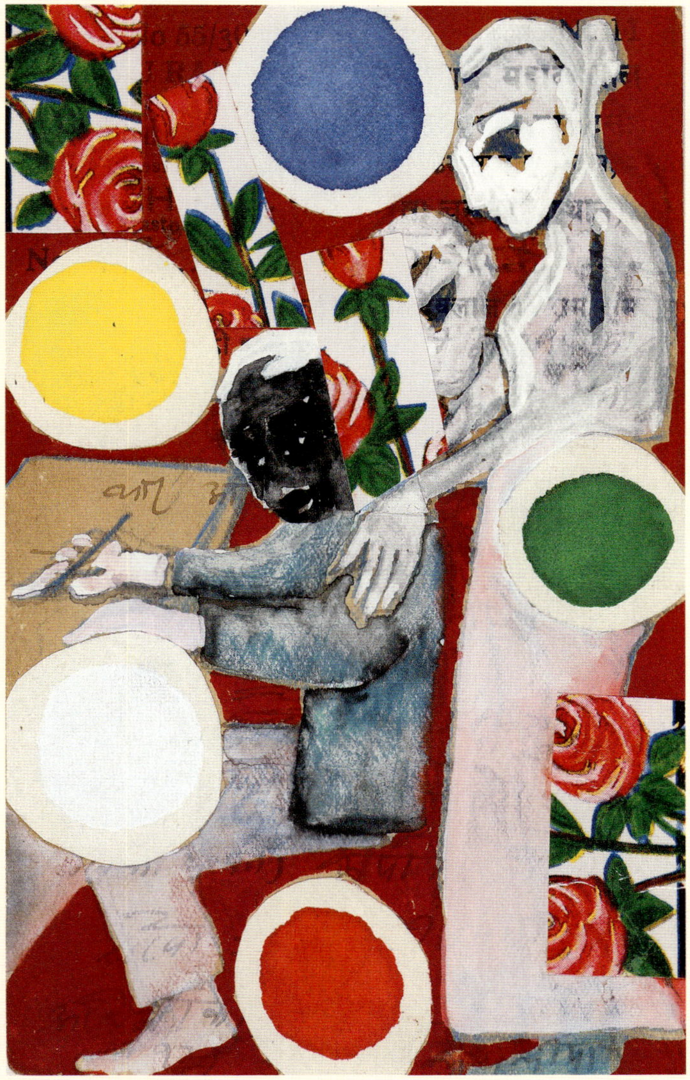

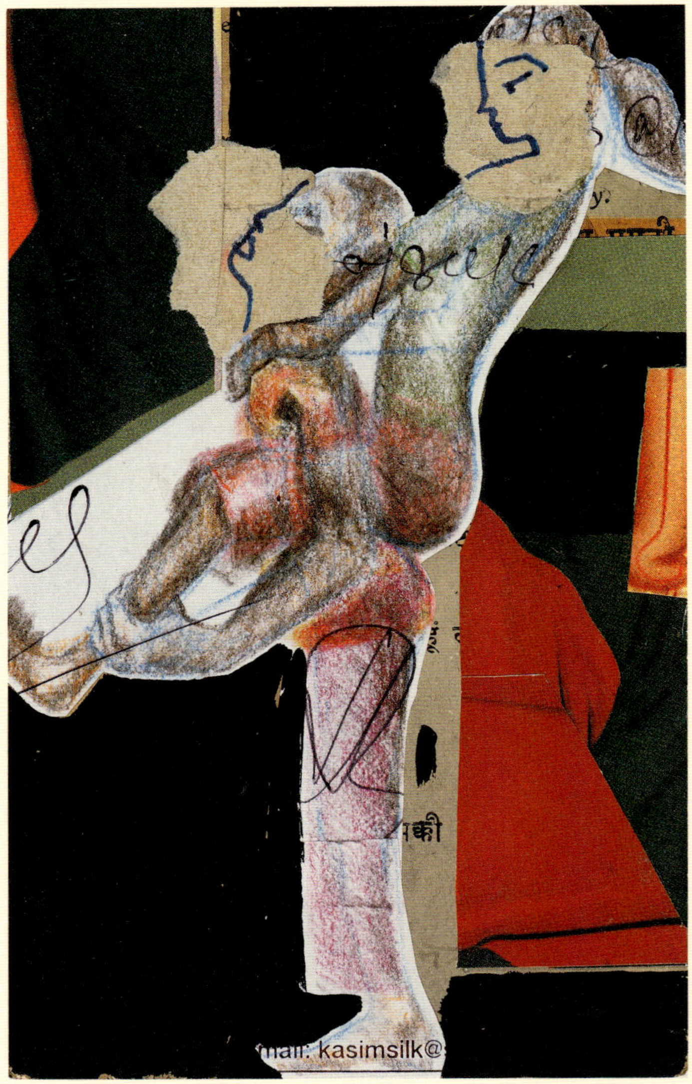
mail: kasimsilk@

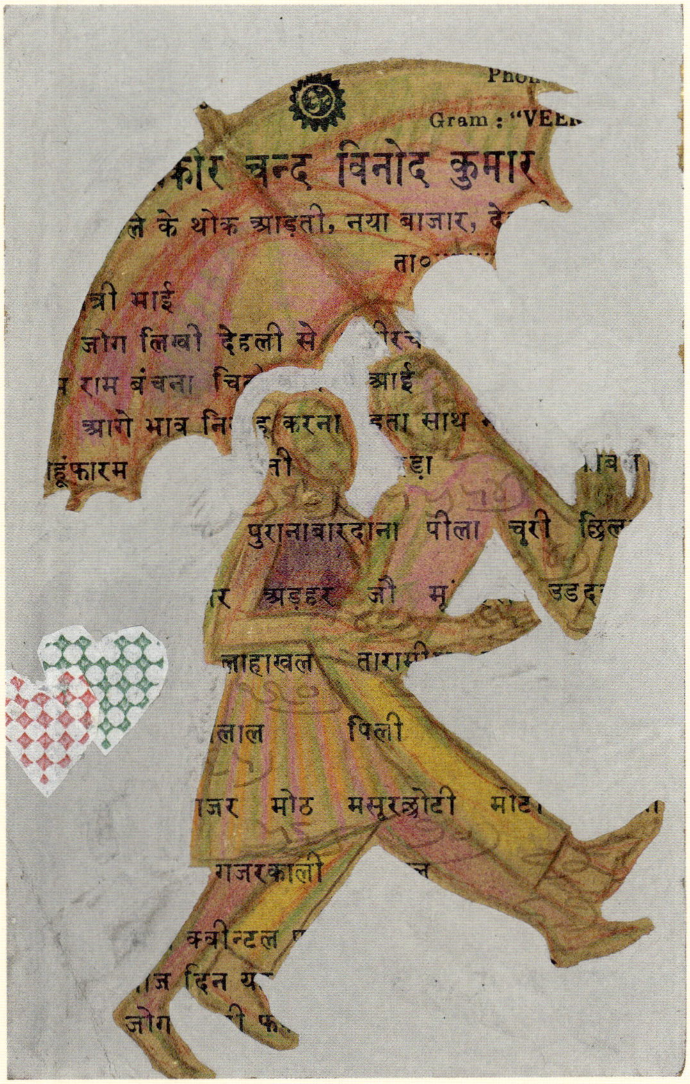

विनोद कुमार
नया बाजार
जोग लिखी देहली से
पुरानाबारदाना पीला चूरी
पिली
गजरकाली

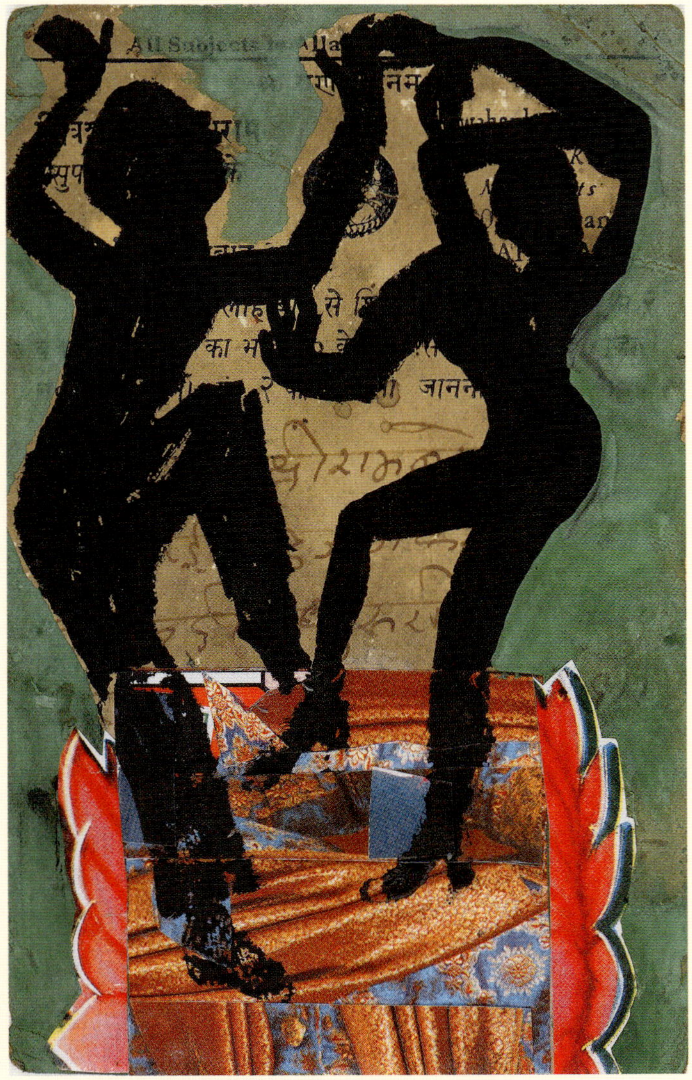

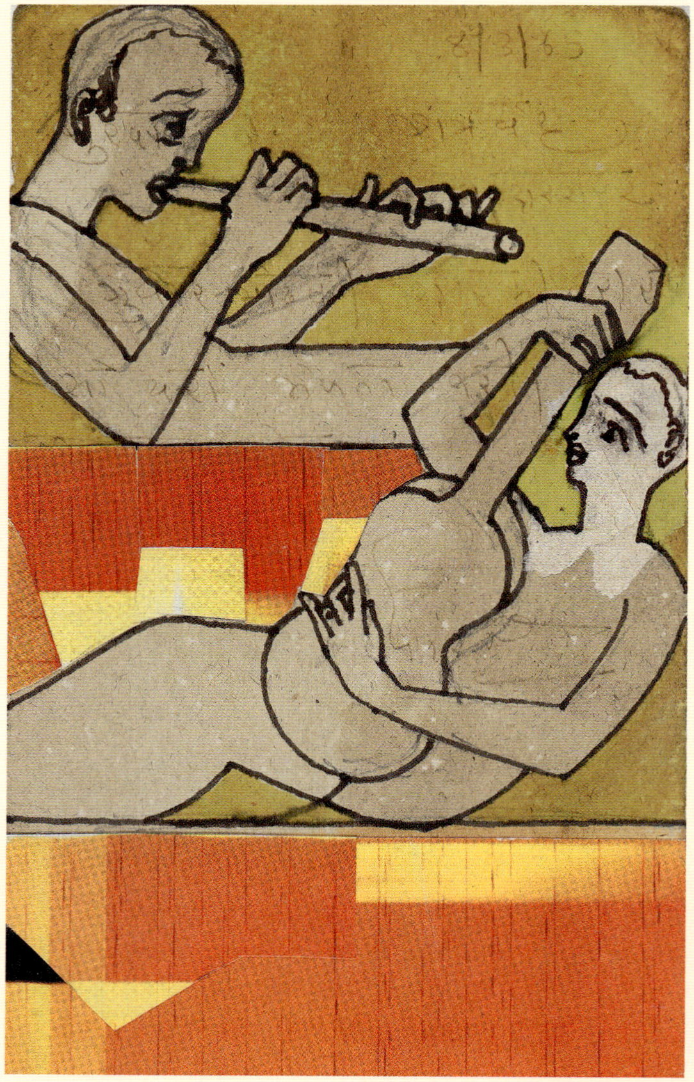

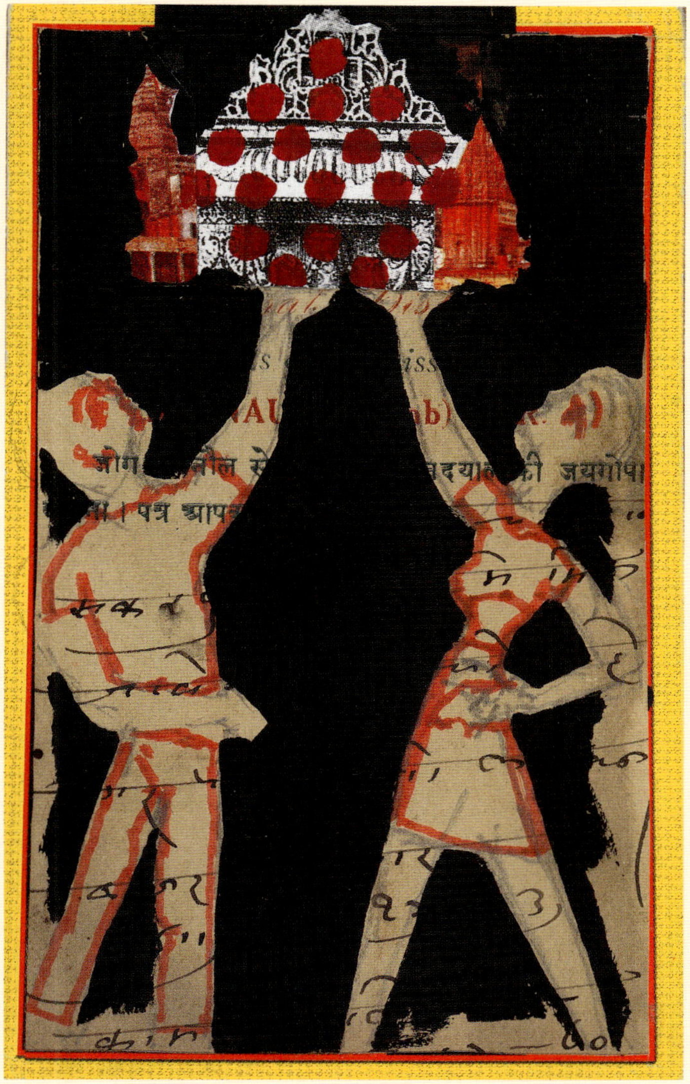

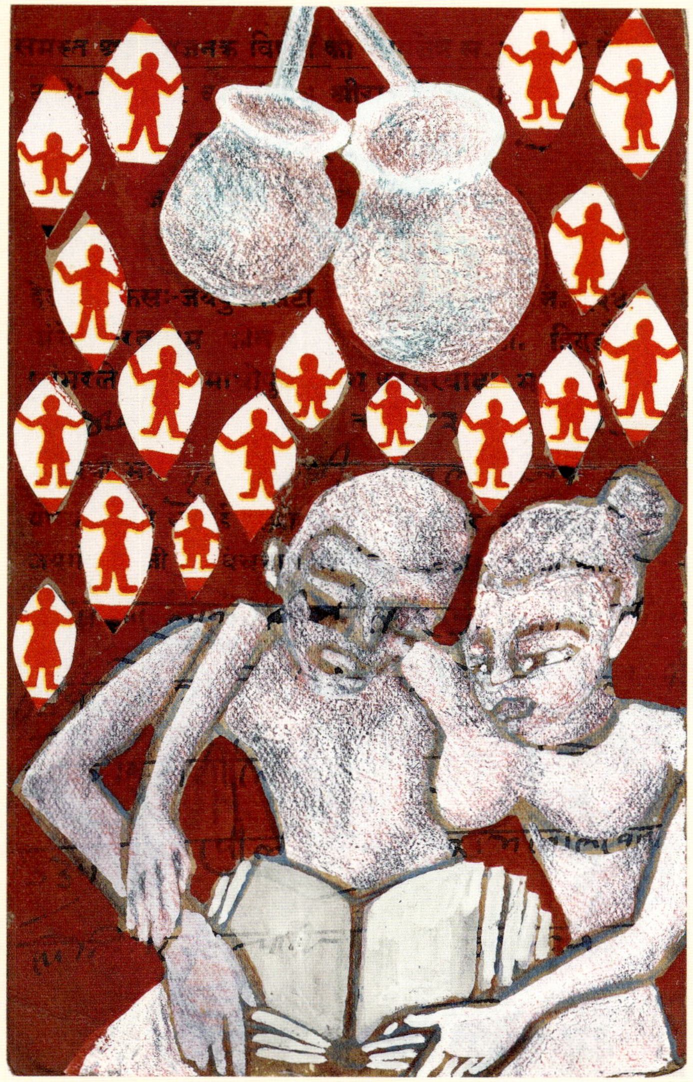

NEW YORK • 2009

SELF-PORTRAITS AS A MAP

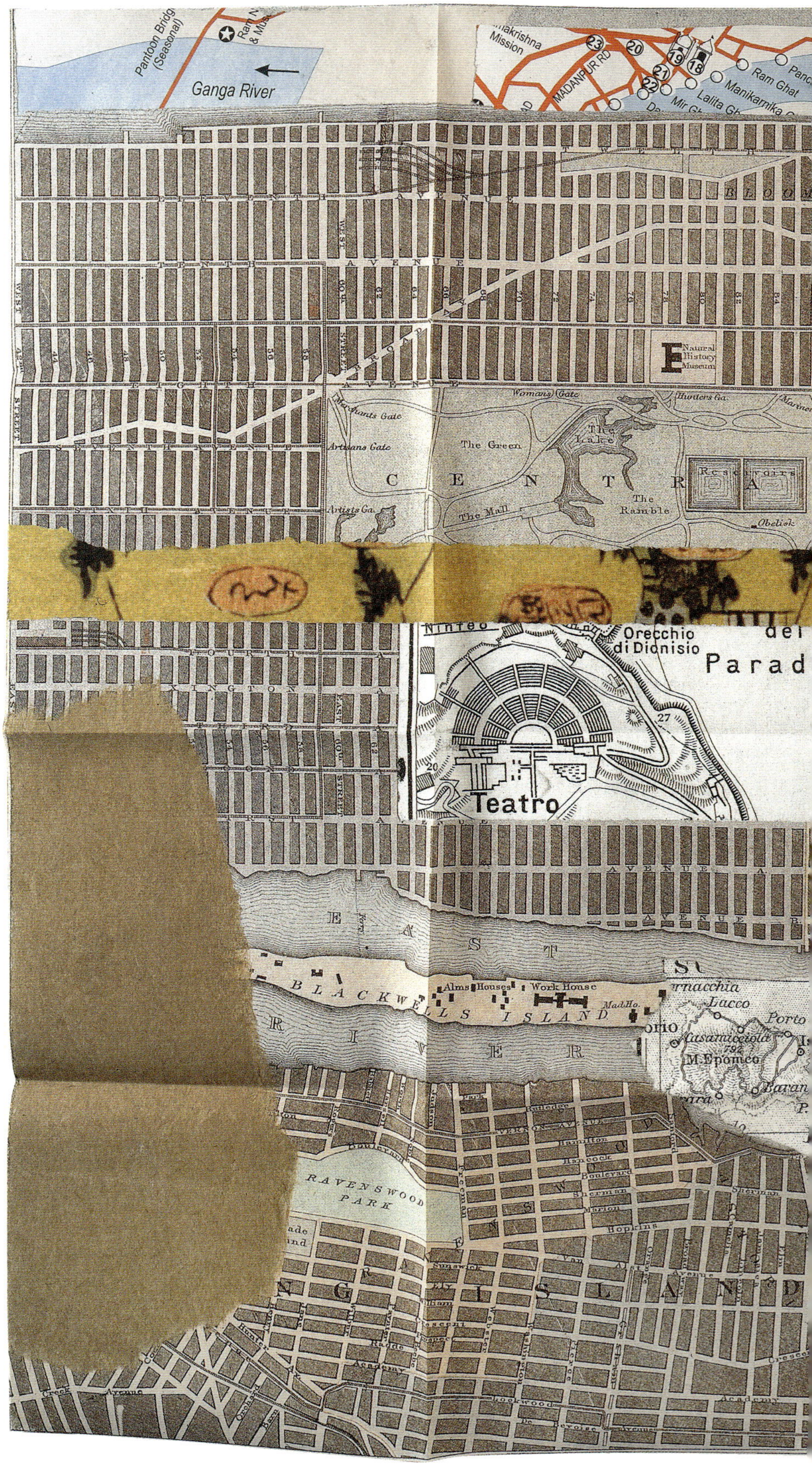
Pantoon Bridg (Seasonal)
Ganga River
Mission
Ram Ghat
Natural History Museum
Womans Gate
Merchants Gate
Artisans Gate
The Green
The Lake
The Mall
The Ramble
Artists Ga.
Obelisk
C E N T R A
Orecchio di Dionisio
Parad
Teatro
Alms Houses
Work House
B L A C K W E L L S I S L A N D
Lacco
Porto
M. Epomeo
R A V E N S W O O D P A R K

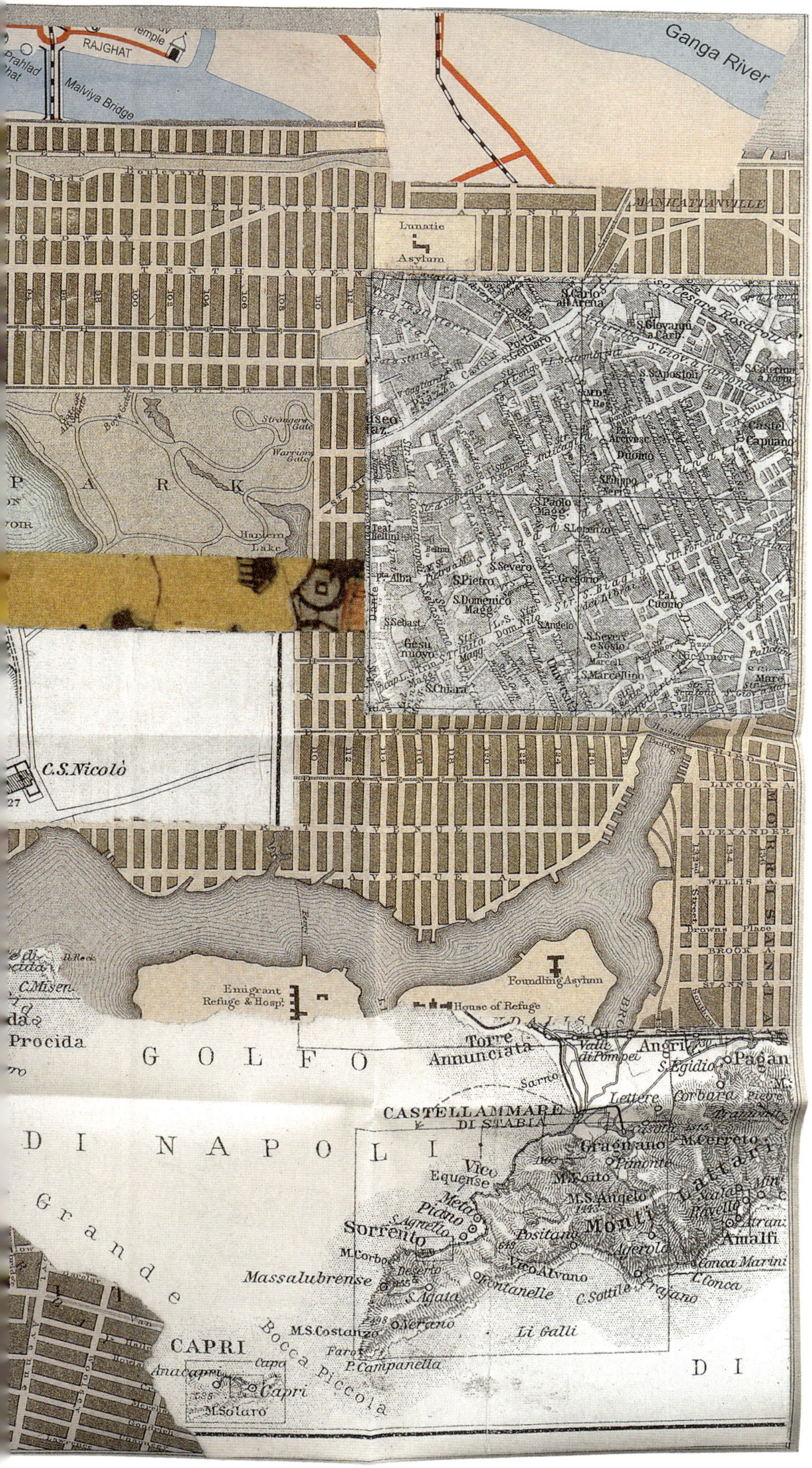
Ganga River
RAJGHAT
Malviya Bridge
Prahlad
Lunatic
Asylum
MANHATTANVILLE
TENTH AVENUE
P A R K
Harlem Lake
Stranger's Gate
Warriors Gate
S.Carlo all'Arena
S.Giovanni a Carb.
Porta S.Gennaro
S.S.Apostoli
Castel Capuano
Arcivesc.
Duomo
S.Filippo Neri
S.Paolo Magg.
S.Lorenzo
S.Severo
S.Pietro
S.Domenico Magg.
Gregorio
S.Chiara
Gesù nuovo
S.Angelo
S.Marcellino
C.S.Nicolò
FIRST AVENUE
LINCOLN A.
ALEXANDER
WILLIS A.
Browns Place
BROOK A.
Emigrant Refuge & Hosp.
Foundling Asylum
House of Refuge
Procida
C.Miseno
G O L F O
D I N A P O L I
Torre Annunciata
Valle di Pompei
Angri
Pagani
S.Egidio
Sarno
CASTELLAMMARE DI STABIA
Lettere
Corbara
Gragnano
M.Cerreto
Pimonte
Vico Equense
M.Faito
Monti Lattari
M.S.Angelo
Meta
Piano
Sorrento
Positano
Agerola
Ravello
Atrani
Amalfi
Conca Marini
Massalubrense
S.Agata
Vico Alvano
Fontanelle
C.Sottile
Li Galli
M.S.Costanzo
Nerano
P.Campanella
CAPRI
Anacapri
Capri
M.Solaro
Bocca Piccola
Grande
D I

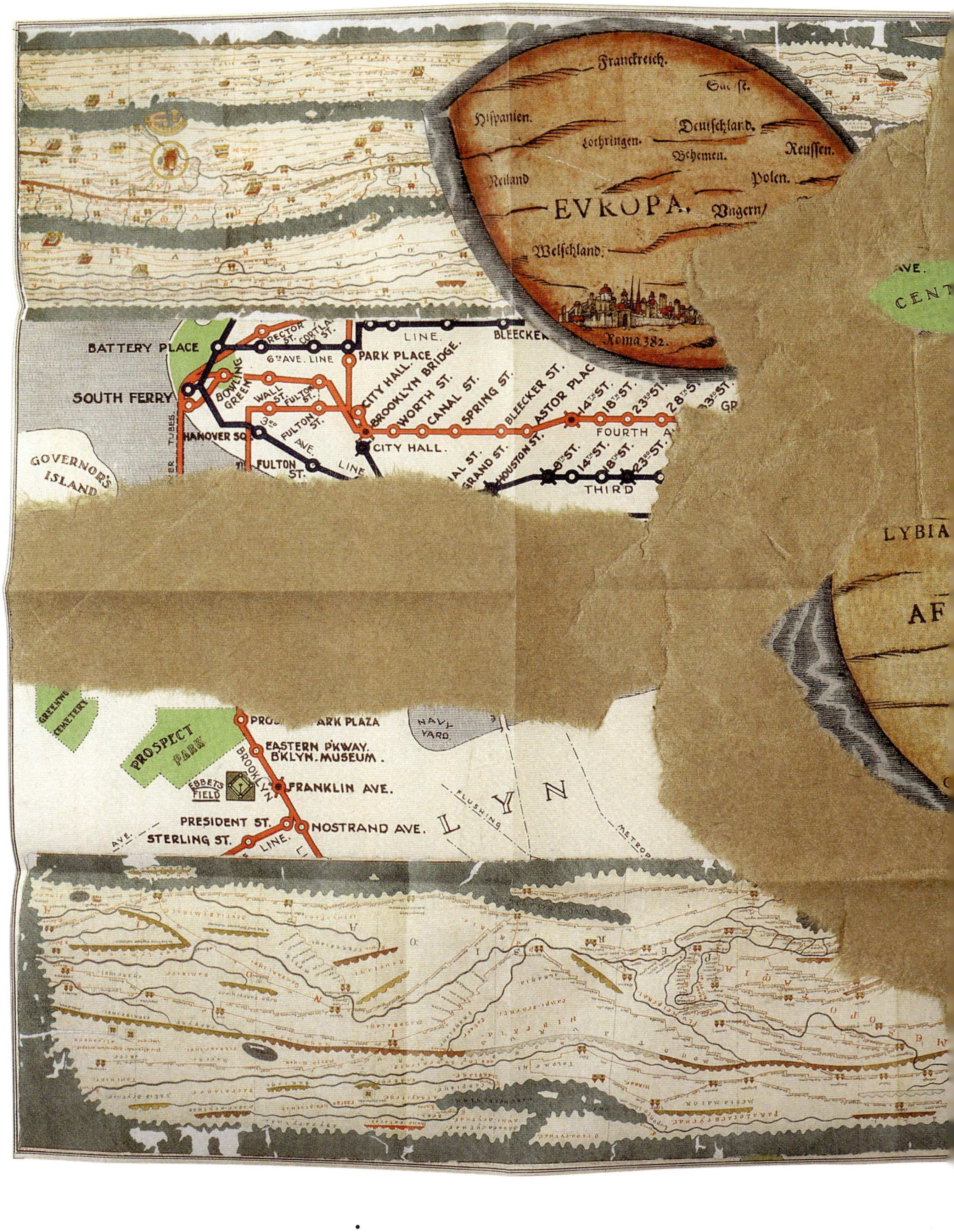
Franckreich.
Hispanien.
Deutschland.
Lothringen.
Behemen.
Reussen.
Meiland
Polen.
EVROPA.
Ungern/
Welschland.
Roma 382.
BATTERY PLACE
SOUTH FERRY
GOVERNOR'S ISLAND
HANOVER SQ
6TH AVE. LINE
PARK PLACE
CITY HALL
BROOKLYN BRIDGE
WORTH ST.
CANAL ST.
SPRING ST.
BLEECKER ST.
ASTOR PLAC
FOURTH
THIRD
BLEECKER
LYBIA
AF
PROSPECT PARK
EASTERN P'KWAY.
BKLYN. MUSEUM.
EBBETS FIELD
FRANKLIN AVE.
PRESIDENT ST.
STERLING ST.
NOSTRAND AVE.
NAVY YARD
L Y N
FLUSHING

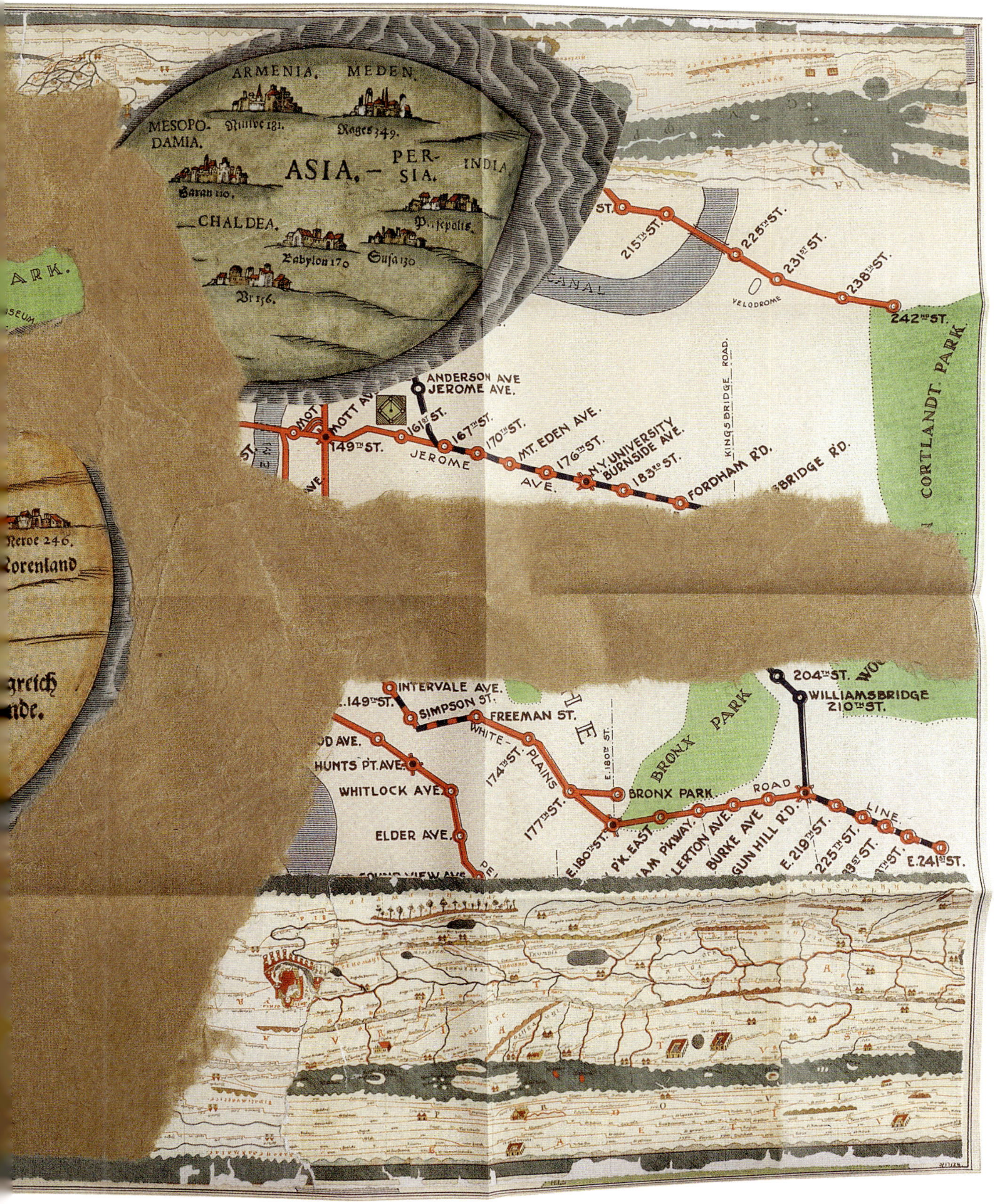

ARMENIA.
MEDEN.
MESOPO-DAMIA.
ASIA.
PER-SIA.
INDIA
CHALDEA.
CANAL
VELODROME
215TH ST.
225TH ST.
231ST ST.
238TH ST.
242ND ST.
CORTLANDT PARK
ANDERSON AVE
JEROME AVE.
MOTT AVE.
149TH ST.
161ST ST.
167TH ST.
170TH ST.
MT. EDEN AVE.
176TH ST.
N.Y. UNIVERSITY
BURNSIDE AVE.
183RD ST.
FORDHAM R'D.
KINGSBRIDGE ROAD.
JEROME AVE.
Meroe 246.
Morenland
INTERVALE AVE.
E.149TH ST.
SIMPSON ST.
FREEMAN ST.
WHITE-PLAINS
HUNTS PT. AVE.
WHITLOCK AVE.
ELDER AVE.
174TH ST.
177TH ST.
E.180TH ST.
BRONX PARK
204TH ST.
WILLIAMSBRIDGE
210TH ST.
ROAD
LINE
BURKE AVE
GUN HILL R'D.
E.219TH ST.
225TH ST.
E.241ST ST.

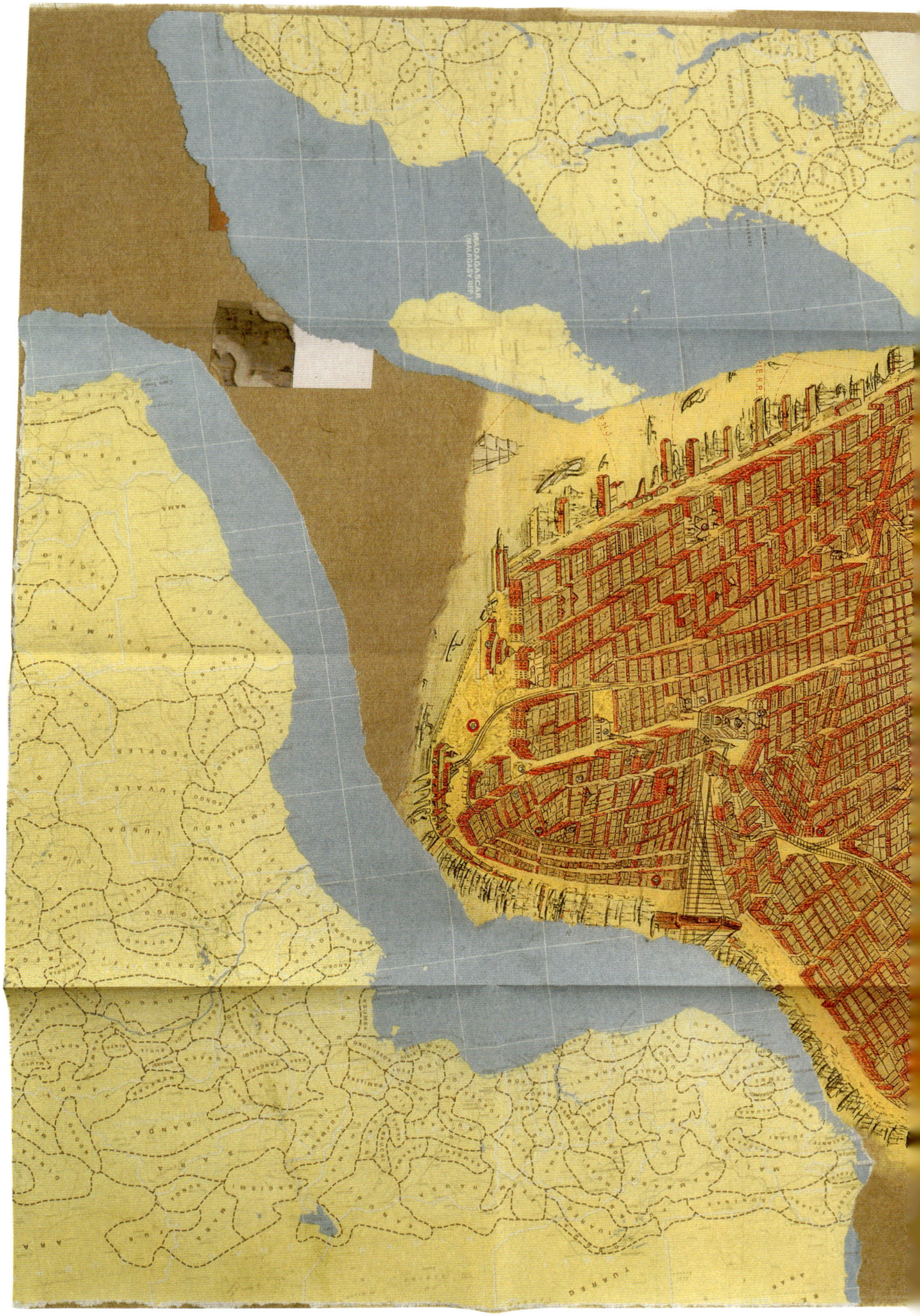

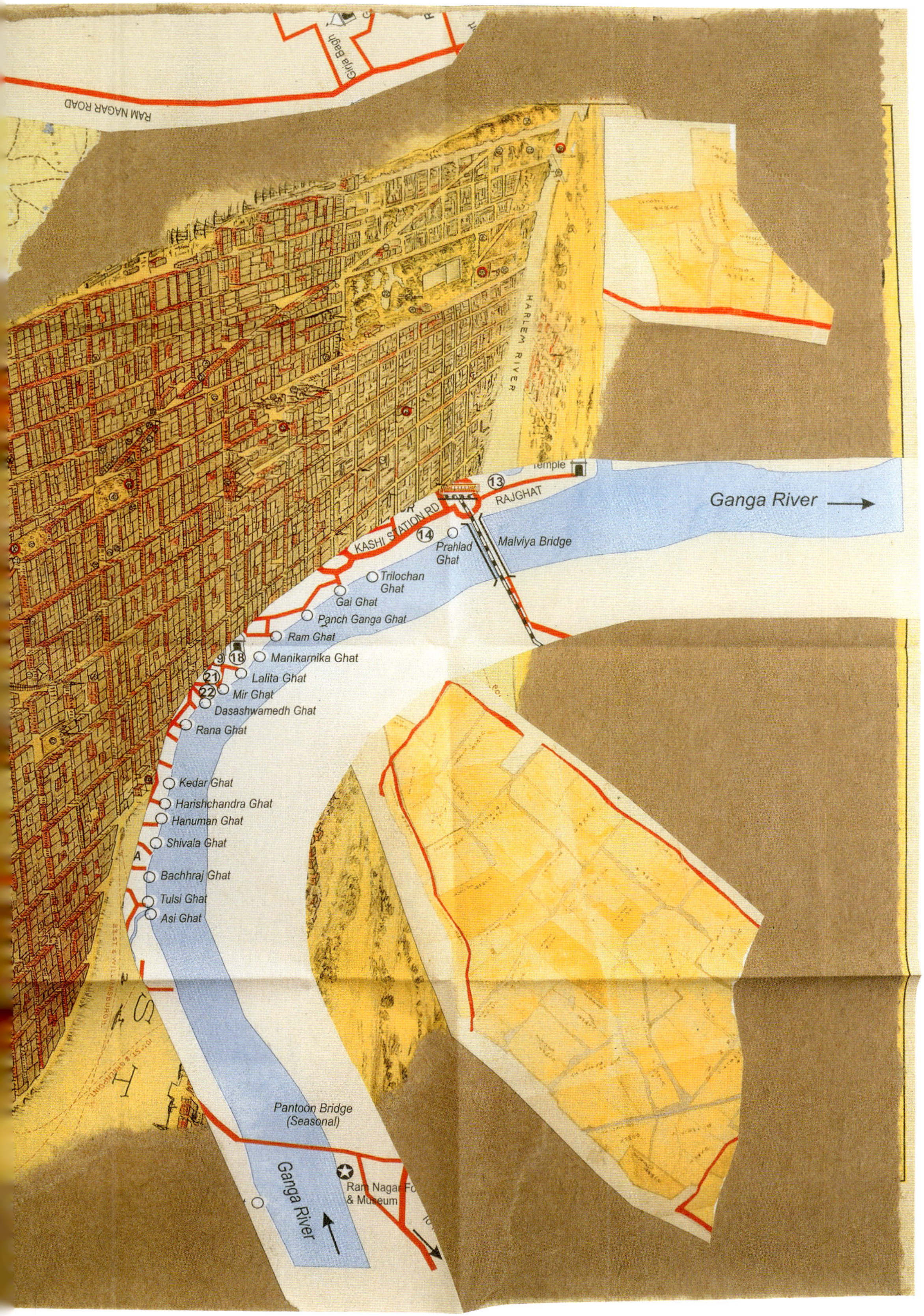

RAM NAGAR ROAD
Girja Bagh
HARLEM RIVER
Temple
13
RAJGHAT
Ganga River
KASHI STATION RD
14
Prahlad Ghat
Malviya Bridge
Trilochan Ghat
Gai Ghat
Panch Ganga Ghat
Ram Ghat
9
18
Manikarnika Ghat
21
Lalita Ghat
22
Mir Ghat
Dasashwamedh Ghat
Rana Ghat
Kedar Ghat
Harishchandra Ghat
Hanuman Ghat
Shivala Ghat
Bachhraj Ghat
Tulsi Ghat
Asi Ghat
Pantoon Bridge (Seasonal)
Ganga River
Ram Nagar Fo
& Museum

L'ORIENT • 2010

AFTER ATTAR'S "THE CONFERENCE OF THE BIRDS"

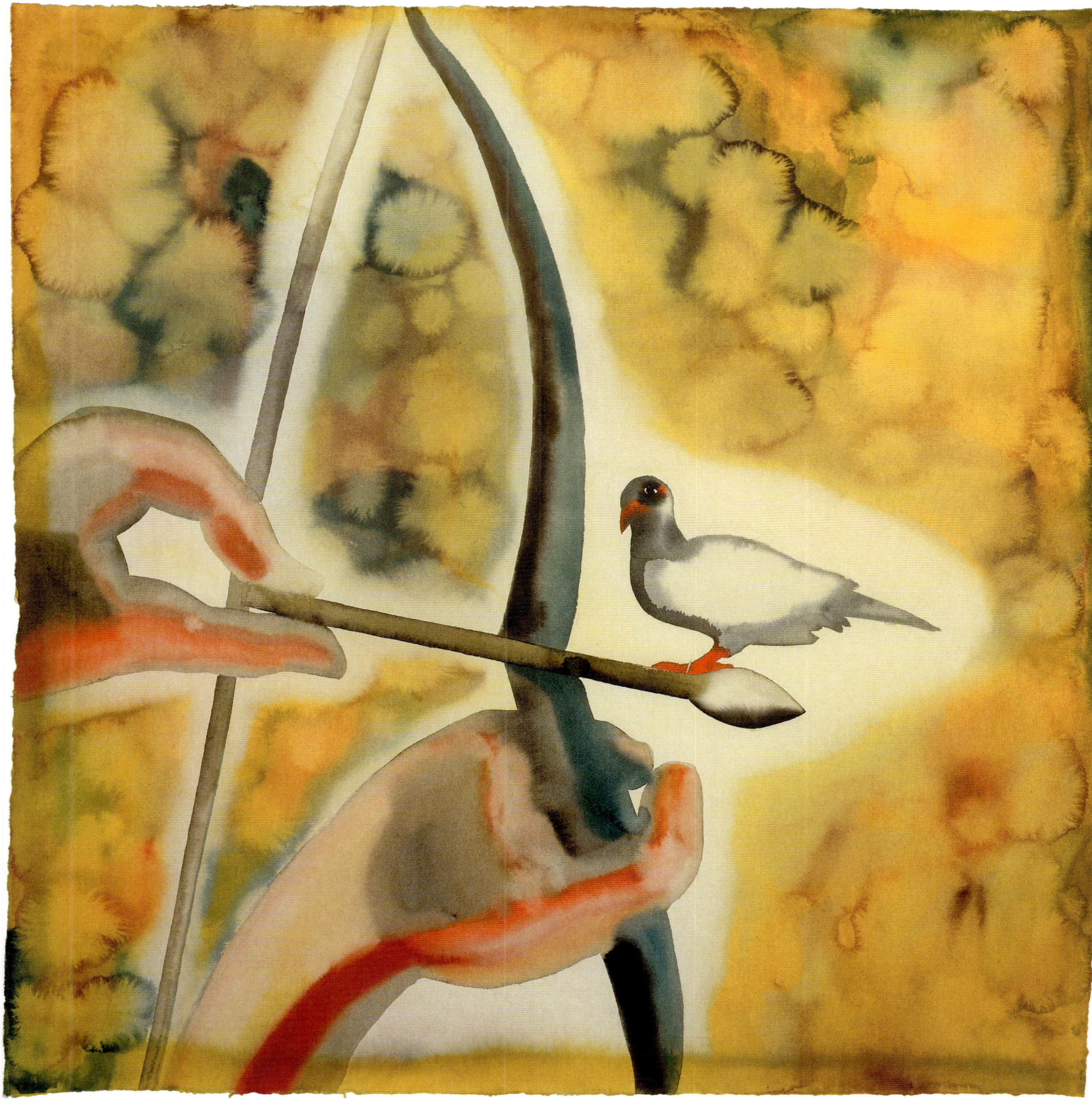

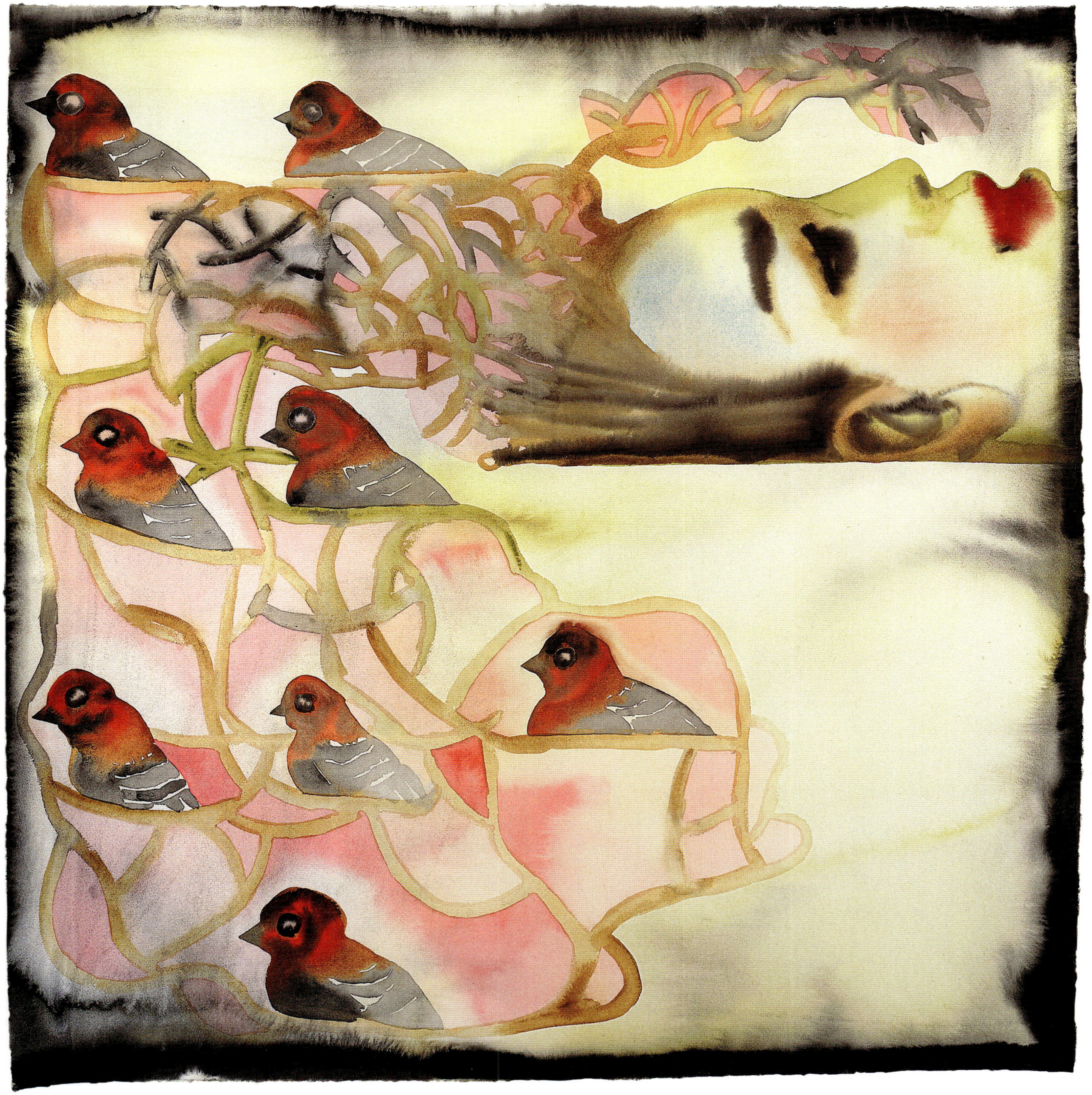

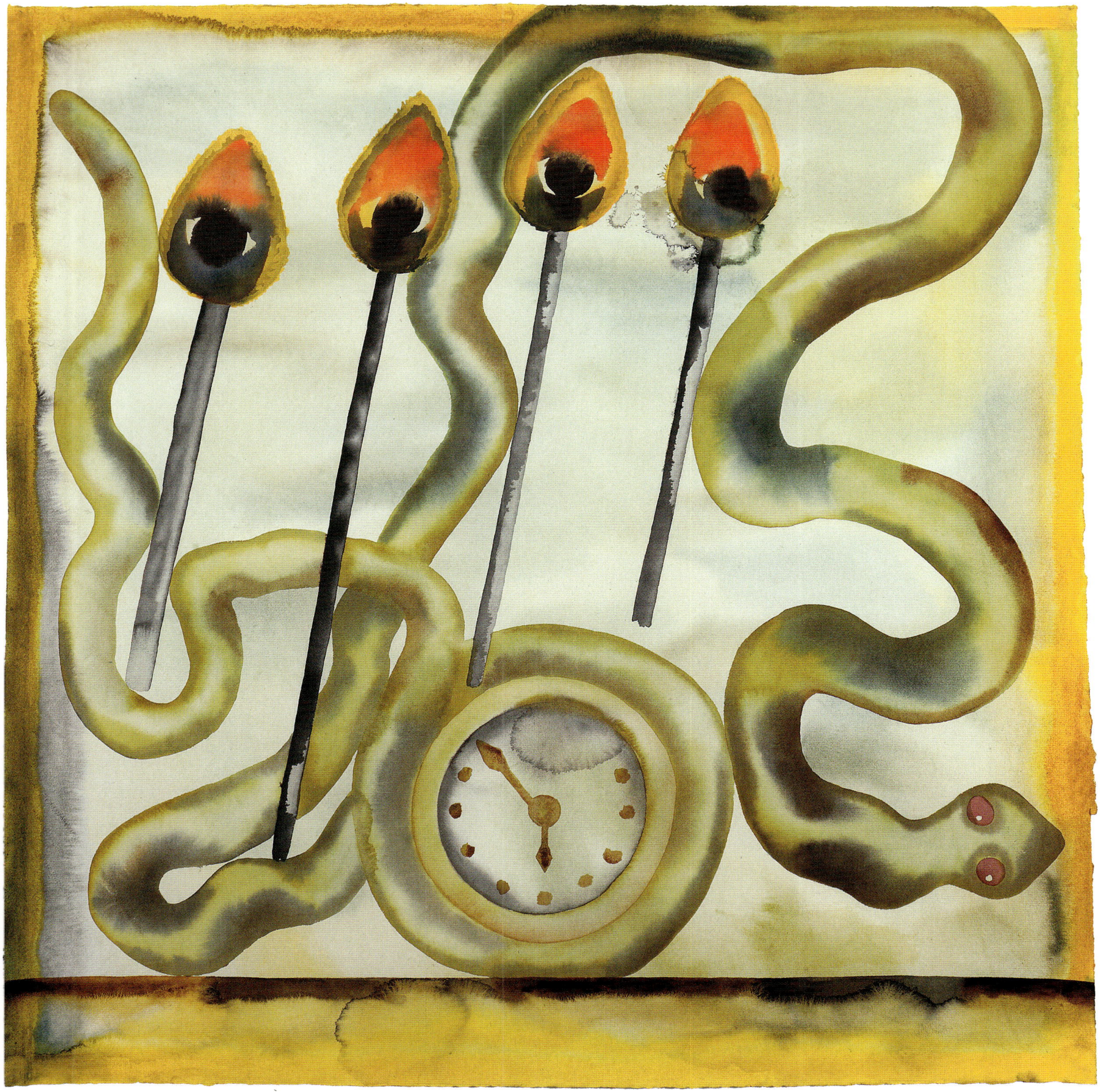

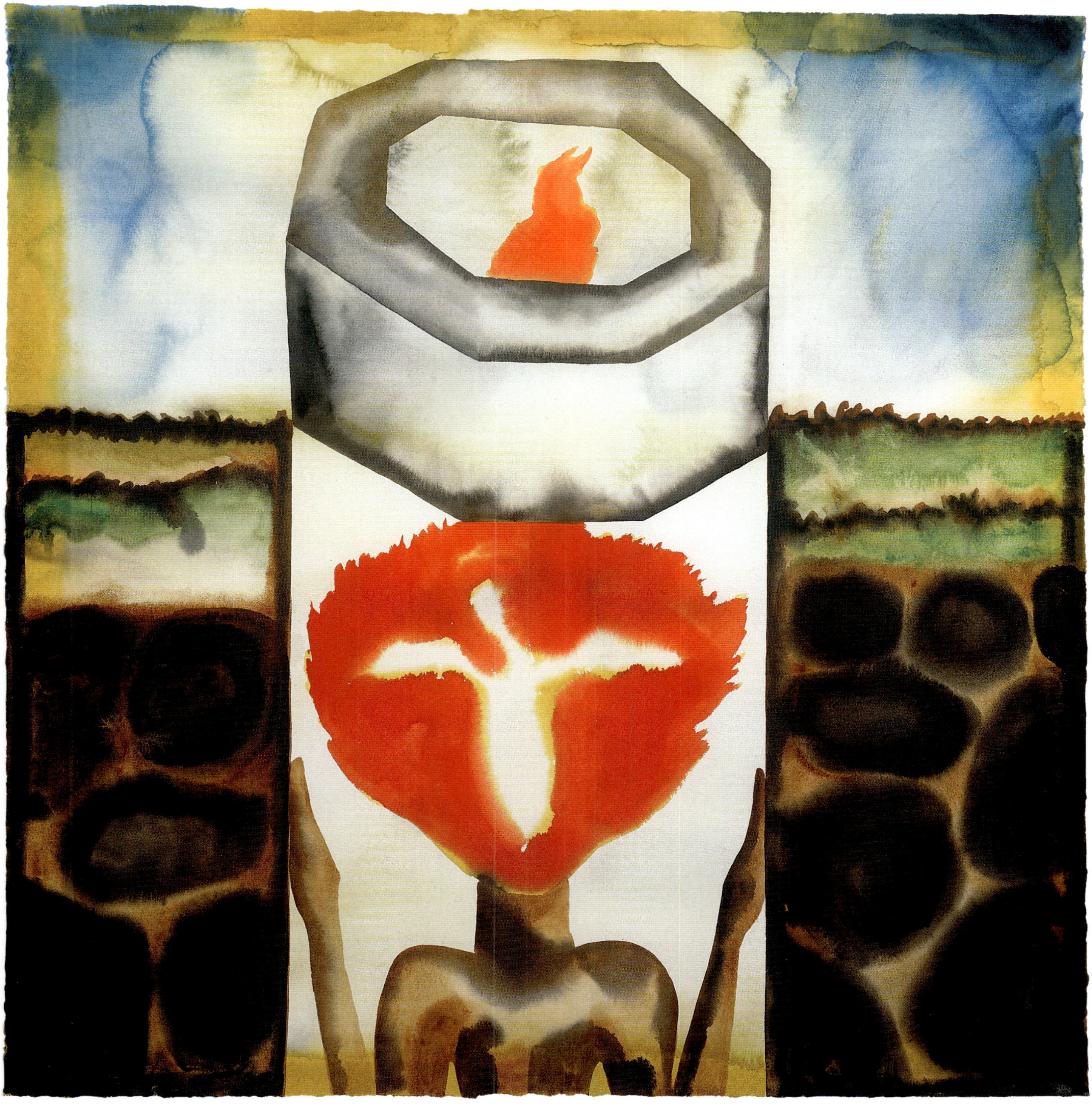

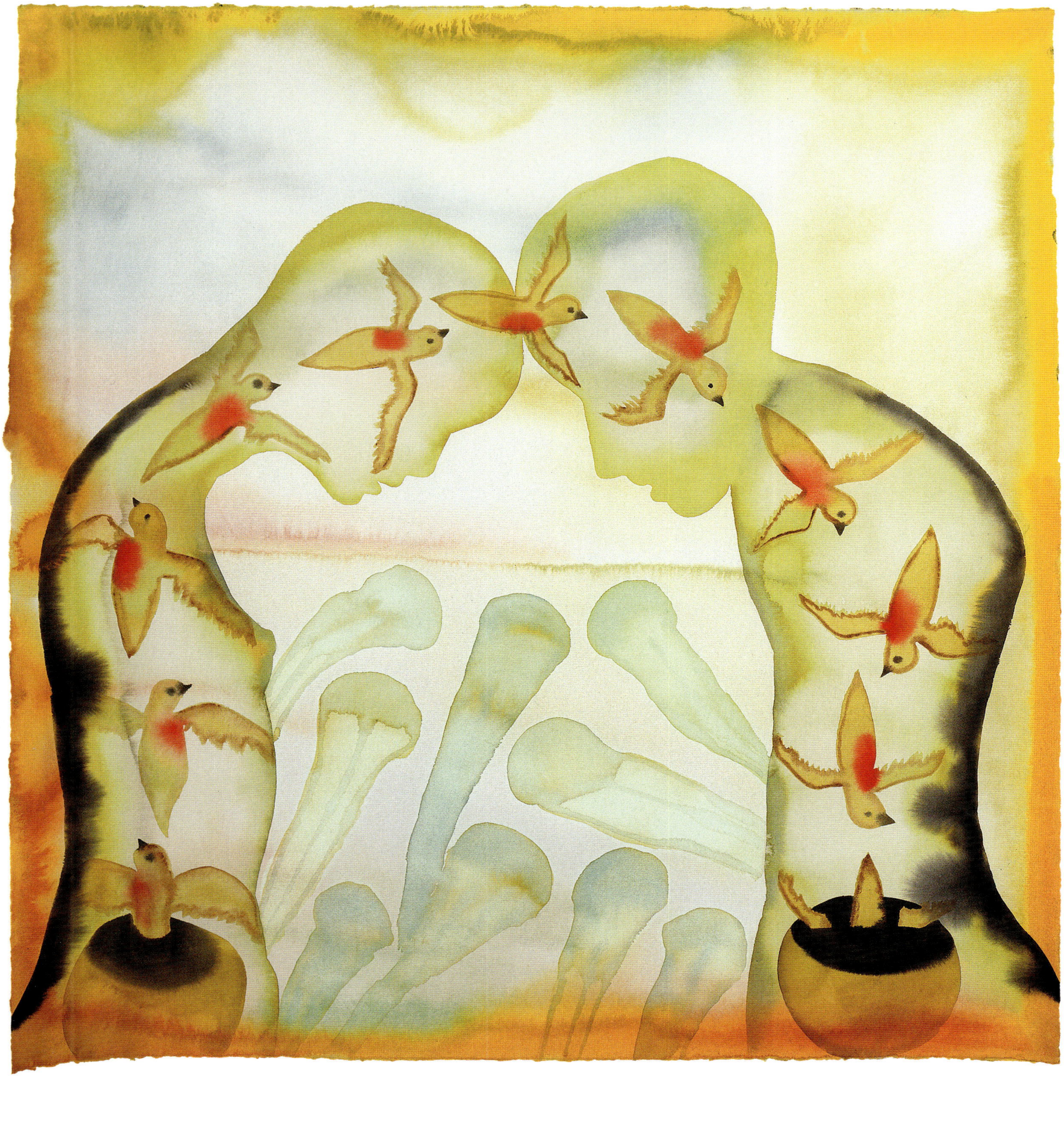

NEW YORK • 2010

IRONS AND RAINBOWS

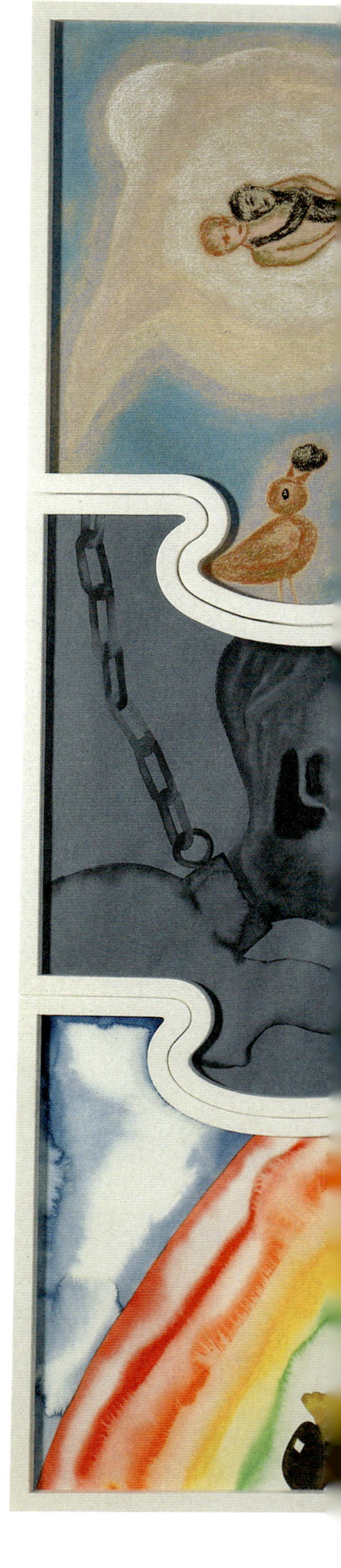

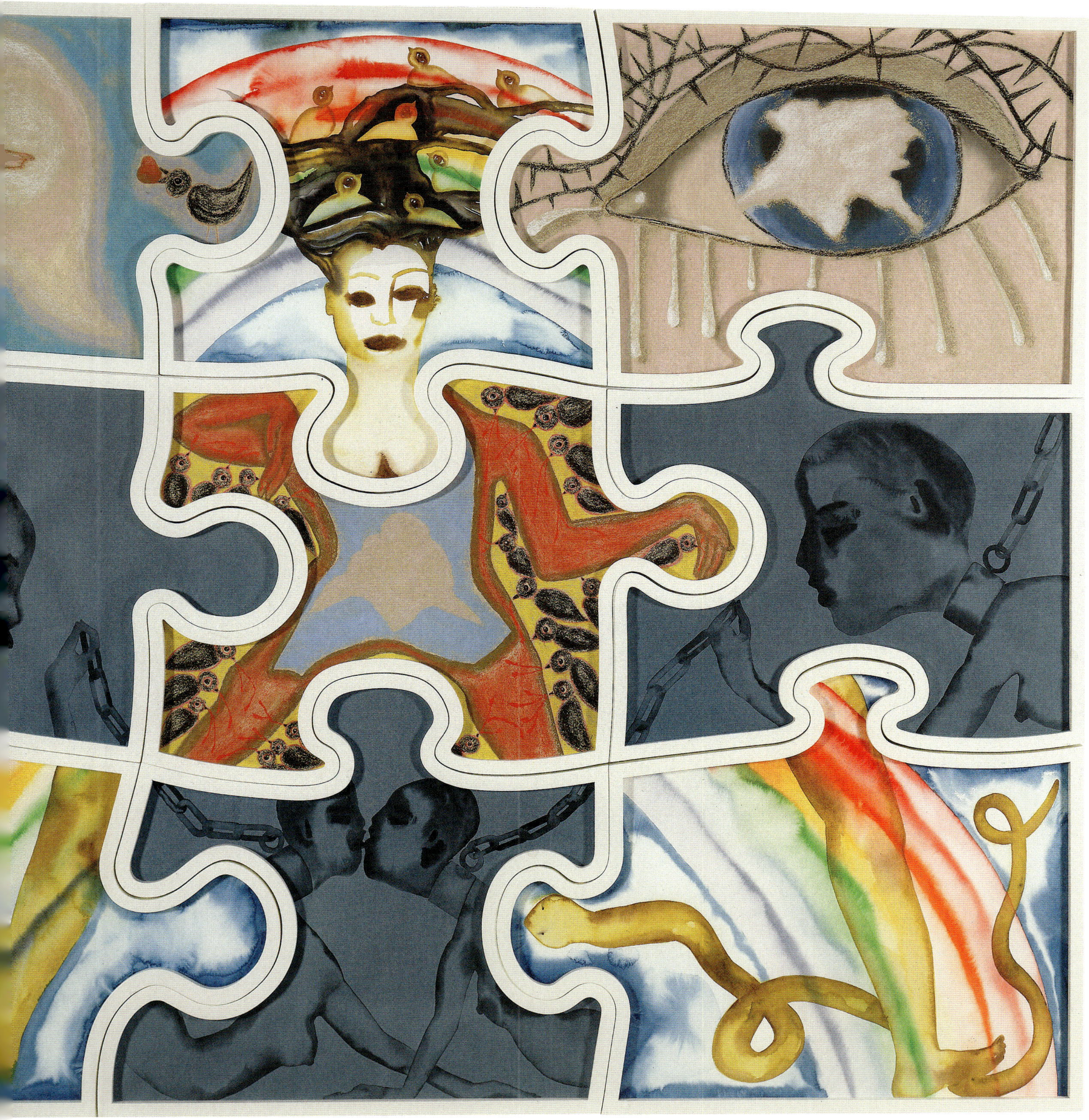

APPENDIX

LIST OF WORKS

Actors of the Terreiro I, 2006
24 x 18 1/8 in. • 61 x 46 cm
Watercolor on paper
Rio de Janeiro, Brazil
p. 14

Actors of the Terreiro II, 2006
24 x 18 1/8 in. • 61 x 46 cm
Watercolor on paper
Rio de Janeiro, Brazil
p. 15

Actors of the Terreiro III, 2006
24 x 18 1/8 in. • 61 x 46 cm
Watercolor on paper
Rio de Janeiro, Brazil
p. 16

Actors of the Terreiro IV, 2006
24 x 18 1/8 in. • 61 x 46 cm
Watercolor on paper
Rio de Janeiro, Brazil
p. 17

Actors of the Terreiro V, 2006
24 x 18 1/8 in. • 61 x 46 cm
Watercolor on paper
Rio de Janeiro, Brazil
p. 18

Actors of the Terreiro VI, 2006
24 x 18 1/8 in. • 61 x 46 cm
Watercolor on paper
Rio de Janeiro, Brazil
p. 19

Actors of the Terreiro VII, 2006
24 x 18 1/8 in. • 61 x 46 cm
Watercolor on paper
Rio de Janeiro, Brazil
p. 20

Actors of the Terreiro VIII, 2007
24 x 18 1/8 in. • 61 x 46 cm
Watercolor on paper
Rio de Janeiro, Brazil
p. 21

Actors of the Terreiro IX, 2007
24 x 18 1/8 in. • 61 x 46 cm
Watercolor on paper
Rio de Janeiro, Brazil
p. 22

Actors of the Terreiro X, 2007
24 x 18 1/8 in. • 61 x 46 cm
Watercolor on paper
Rio de Janeiro, Brazil
p. 23

Actors of the Terreiro XI, 2007
24 x 18 1/8 in. • 61 x 46 cm
Watercolor on paper
Rio de Janeiro, Brazil
p. 24

Actors of the Terreiro XII, 2007
24 x 18 1/8 in. • 61 x 46 cm
Watercolor on paper
Bahia, Brazil
p. 25

Actors of the Terreiro XIII, 2008
24 x 18 1/8 in. • 61 x 46 cm
Watercolor on paper
Bahia, Brazil
p. 26

Actors of the Terreiro XIV, 2008
24 x 18 1/8 in. • 61 x 46 cm
Watercolor on paper
Bahia, Brazil
p. 27

Twenty-One Kinds of Love I, 2008
5.5 x 3.54 in. • 14 x 9 cm
Pencil, watercolor, ink, tempera
and collage on paper
Varanasi, India
p. 30

Twenty-One Kinds of Love II, 2008
5.5 x 3.54 in. • 14 x 9 cm
Pencil, watercolor, ink, tempera
and collage on paper
Varanasi, India
p. 31

Twenty-One Kinds of Love III, 2008
5.5 x 3.54 in. • 14 x 9 cm
Pencil, watercolor, ink, tempera
and collage on paper
Varanasi, India
p. 31

Twenty-One Kinds of Love IV, 2008
5.5 x 3.54 in. • 14 x 9 cm
Pencil, watercolor, ink, tempera
and collage on paper
Varanasi, India
p. 32

Twenty-One Kinds of Love V, 2008
5.5 x 3.54 in. • 14 x 9 cm
Pencil, watercolor, ink, tempera
and collage on paper
Varanasi, India
p. 33

Twenty-One Kinds of Love VI, 2008
5.5 x 3.54 in. • 14 x 9 cm
Pencil, watercolor, ink, tempera
and collage on paper
Varanasi, India
p. 33

Twenty-One Kinds of Love VII, 2008
5.5 x 3.54 in. • 14 x 9 cm
Pencil, watercolor, ink, tempera
and collage on paper
Varanasi, India
p. 34

Twenty-One Kinds of Love VIII, 2008
5.5 x 3.54 in. • 14 x 9 cm
Pencil, watercolor, ink, tempera
and collage on paper
Varanasi, India
p. 35

Twenty-One Kinds of Love IX, 2008
5.5 x 3.54 in. • 14 x 9 cm
Pencil, watercolor, ink, tempera
and collage on paper
Varanasi, India
p. 35

Twenty-One Kinds of Love X, 2008
5.5 x 3.54 in. • 14 x 9 cm
Pencil, watercolor, ink, tempera
and collage on paper
Varanasi, India
p. 36

Twenty-One Kinds of Love XI, 2008
5.5 x 3.54 in. • 14 x 9 cm
Pencil, watercolor, ink, tempera
and collage on paper
Varanasi, India
p. 37

Twenty-One Kinds of Love XII, 2008
5.5 x 3.54 in. • 14 x 9 cm
Pencil, watercolor, ink, tempera
and collage on paper
Varanasi, India
p. 37

Twenty-One Kinds of Love XIII, 2008
5.5 x 3.54 in. • 14 x 9 cm
Pencil, watercolor, ink, tempera
and collage on paper
Varanasi, India
p. 38

Twenty-One Kinds of Love XIV, 2008
5.5 x 3.54 in. • 14 x 9 cm
Pencil, watercolor, ink, tempera
and collage on paper
Varanasi, India
p. 39

Twenty-One Kinds of Love XV, 2008
5.5 x 3.54 in. • 14 x 9 cm
Pencil, watercolor, ink, tempera
and collage on paper
Varanasi, India
p. 39

Twenty-One Kinds of Love XVI, 2008
5.5 x 3.54 in. • 14 x 9 cm
Pencil, watercolor, ink, tempera
and collage on paper
Varanasi, India
p. 40

Twenty-One Kinds of Love XVII, 2008
5.5 x 3.54 in. • 14 x 9 cm
Pencil, watercolor, ink, tempera
and collage on paper
Varanasi, India
p. 41

Twenty-One Kinds of Love XVIII, 2008
5.5 x 3.54 in. • 14 x 9 cm
Pencil, watercolor, ink, tempera
and collage on paper
Varanasi, India
p. 41

Twenty-One Kinds of Love XIX, 2008
5.5 x 3.54 in. • 14 x 9 cm
Pencil, watercolor, ink, tempera
and collage on paper
Varanasi, India
p. 42

Twenty-One Kinds of Love XX, 2008
5.5 x 3.54 in. • 14 x 9 cm
Pencil, watercolor, ink, tempera
and collage on paper
Varanasi, India
p. 43

Twenty-One Kinds of Love XXI, 2008
5.5 x 3.54 in. • 14 x 9 cm
Pencil, watercolor, ink, tempera
and collage on paper
Varanasi, India
p. 43

—

Self-Portrait as a Map I, 2009
65.46 x 78.5 in. • 166.27 x 199.39 cm
Ink and collaged paper
New York, U.S.A.
pp. 46-47

Self Portrait as a Map II, 2009
45.34 x 78.5 in. • 115.16 x 199.39 cm
Ink and collaged paper
New York, U.S.A.
pp. 48-49

Self Portrait as a Map III, 2009
55.5 x 80.5 inches • 140.97 x 204.47 cm
Ink and collaged paper
New York, U.S.A.
pp. 50-51

—

After Attar's "The Conference of the Birds" I, 2010
45 x 45 in. • 114.3 x 114.3 cm
Watercolor on paper
L'Orient, French West Indies
p. 55

After Attar's "The Conference of the Birds" II, 2010
45 x 45 in. • 114.3 x 114.3 cm
Watercolor on paper
L'Orient, French West Indies
p. 57

After Attar's "The Conference of the Birds" III, 2010
45 x 45 in. • 114.3 x 114.3 cm
Watercolor on paper
L'Orient, French West Indies
p. 59

After Attar's "The Conference of the Birds" IV, 2010
45 x 45 in. • 114.3 x 114.3 cm
Watercolor on paper
L'Orient, French West Indies
p. 61

After Attar's "The Conference of the Birds" V, 2010
45 x 45 in. • 114.3 x 114.3 cm
Watercolor on paper
L'Orient, French West Indies
p. 63

—

Irons and Rainbows, 2010
77 x 98 in. • 195.58 x 248.92 cm
Pastel and watercolor on paper
New York, U.S.A.
pp. 66-67

BIOGRAPHY

Francesco Clemente's oeuvre spans four decades and has achieved international acclaim.

Throughout the 1970s he exhibited works that reflected his interest in the contemplative traditions of India, where he lived for several years.

In 1981 Clemente moved to New York with his wife, Alba, and their four children.
His paintings, drawings, prints and illustrated books were featured in shows at numerous international venues including the Whitechapel Art Gallery, London; the Nationalgalerie, Berlin; the Metropolitan Museum of Art, New York; the Art Institute of Chicago; and the Dia Center for the Arts, New York.

Through the 1990s, surveys of his work were exhibited by the Philadelphia Museum of Art; the Royal Academy of the Arts, London; the Pompidou Center, Paris; and the Sezon Museum of Modern Art, Tokyo. In 1999/2000, the Solomon R. Guggenheim Museum in New York and the Guggenheim Bilbao organized a major retrospective of Clemente's work.

More recently his works were exhibited by the Irish Museum of Modern Art, Dublin (2004); The Rose Art Museum, Waltham, Massachusetts (2004); Museo Maxxi, Rome (2006) and Museo MADRE, Naples (2009).

He has participated in numerous collaborative projects, painting with Jean-Michel Basquiat and Andy Warhol, and illuminating poetry by Robert Creeley, Allen Ginsberg, John Wieners and Rene Ricard.

Clemente is a member of the American Academy of Arts and Letters.

DESIGN Daniela Meda

EDITORIAL COORDINATION Filomena Moscatelli

COPYEDITING Charles Gute

COPYWRITING AND PRESS OFFICE Silvia Palombi

US EDITORIAL DIRECTOR Francesca Sorace

PROMOTION AND WEB Monica D'Emidio

DISTRIBUTION Antonia De Besi

ADMINISTRATION Grazia De Giosa

WAREHOUSE AND OUTLET Roberto Curiale

COVER
Twenty-One Kinds of Love I, 2008

PHOTO CREDITS
Adam Reich
Beth Phillips

We apologize if, due to reasons wholly beyond our control, some of the photo sources have not been listed.

ISBN 978-88-8158-795-7

Printed in Italy

Edizioni Charta srl
Milano
via della Moscova, 27 - 20121
Tel. +39-026598098/026598200
Fax +39-026598577
e-mail: charta@chartaartbooks.it

Charta Books Ltd.
New York City
Tel. +1-3134068468
e-mail: international@chartaartbooks.it

www.chartaartbooks.it

Mary Boone Gallery
745 Fifth Avenue
New York, NY 10151
Tel. +1-2127522929
Fax +1-2127523939
e-mail: info@maryboonegallery.com

This book has been published
on the occasion of

FRANCESCO CLEMENTE
A PRIVATE GEOGRAPHY

October 29 - December 18, 2010
Mary Boone Gallery, New York

The artist would like to thank

Arthur C. Danto
Bill Katz
Jeri Coppola
Lenny Niemeyer
Nessia Pope
Renu and Amit Judge
Ricardo Kugelmas

To find out more about Charta,
and to learn about our most recent
publications, visit

WWW.CHARTAARTBOOKS.IT

Printed in October 2010
by BIANCA&VOLTA, Truccazzano
for Edizioni Charta